FLY-FISHING
Odyssey

THE PURSUIT OF GREAT GAME FISH

Jon B. Cave

Illustrations by Dave Hall

WORLD
PUBLICATIONS

Published by
World Publications
460 N. Orlando Ave., Suite 200
Winter Park, FL 32789
www.worldpub.net

Printed in the United States of America

10 9 8 7 6 5 4 3 2 1

Edited by David Ritchie
Design by Tom McGlinchy
Illustrations by Dave Hall
Gear and fly photos by Doug DuKane
All other photos by Jon B. Cave unless otherwise credited

Library of Congress Cataloging-in-Publication Data
Cave, Jon B., 1946-
  Fly-fishing odyssey : the pursuit of great game fish / Jon B. Cave ;
illustrations by Dave Hall.
      p. cm.
  ISBN 0-944406-50-5 (hardcover)
  1. Fly fishing—Anecdotes. 2. Cave, Jon B., 1946- I. Title.
SH456 .C38 2001
799.1'24—dc21
                                        2001005139

To Mom and Dad,
who led me on my earliest adventures.

ACKNOWLEDGEMENTS

I first brought the idea of this book to David Ritchie, editor of *Fly Fishing in Salt Waters*, in the middle of 2000. He was enthusiastic from the outset, and one year later, with David spearheading the project, *Fly-Fishing Odyssey* came to fruition. Throughout the endeavor, he has been a good friend as well as a supportive adviser.

Tom McGlinchy is responsible for the beautiful and tasteful layout of the book. He is a meticulous, innovative individual who will not accept second best.

Thanks also to the many other professionals at World Publications who helped make this book a reality, including Scott Leon, Nancy Ogburn, Diana Krummel, Lisa Earlywine and Don Hill.

I've long been an admirer of Dave Hall's work and feel fortunate to have his artistic skill grace these pages. He has captured the very essence of each fish and of fly-fishing itself.

Some of the photography comes courtesy of highly talented professionals. Thanks to Neal and Linda Rogers, Cathy and Barry Beck, Timothy O'Keefe, Val Atkinson, Guy Tillotson, Doug DuKane and Bailey Bobbitt.

I'd also like to express my gratitude to Lefty Kreh for his complimentary foreword and the generous assistance he has given me over the years.

A special thanks goes to family and to other friends who have through either their encouragement or companionship on the water also made this book possible.

CONTENTS

FOREWORD

By Lefty Kreh

I don't remember when I first met Jon Cave, but it was a long time ago. What I do remember clearly is that I was immediately impressed with this knowledgeable but soft-spoken fly-fisherman.

Through the years, I've found there are two basic kinds of fly-fishermen/outdoor writers/teachers: those who display their knowledge and those who share it. Those who attempt to demonstrate to their students or others how accomplished they are only put people off. But those who share their knowledge enrich everyone they come in contact with. Jon is a sharer.

As you'll see in this book, Jon has led a rewarding fly-fishing life, traveling to near and distant waters and fishing for a wide variety of species. But this book is much more than just an author sharing his experiences. He gives interesting facts about the habits and prey preferences of each of the fish he seeks. This is invaluable information to a fly-fisherman. Then he recommends from experience the kind of tackle needed, including a list of his favorite flies.

Many of his trips took him to distant places, such as New Zealand, Costa Rica and British Columbia. But Jon also gives meticulous information about many species that can be caught locally.

The appendixes alone are worth the price of the book. They are chock-full of information, such as a travel list, how to get more rods aboard an airplane, how you can build a leader to fit your own fishing conditions and much, much more.

Yes, Jon is one who shares. This book is a unique combination of exciting fishing tales and priceless information that any fly-fisherman can profit from. I recommend this book to anyone who loves the sport. You'll find it not only a pleasure to read, but also a tool to increase your knowledge and improve your skills.

INTRODUCTION

By Jon B. Cave

In the sport we call fly-fishing, it's often the means that justify the end. That's because fly-fishing is much more than the act of catching a fish with a fly. It's about salmon clearing a powerful rapid in pursuit of ancestral breeding grounds, humpback whales breaching in a bay near a school of roosterfish or traditional Mosquito Indian women washing clothes in a remote Honduran coastal river. It's about making that perfect cast to a particularly wary or selective fish, the apprehensions and satisfactions that come with buying a new skiff and the pleasures of an exquisitely engineered rod matched to a jewellike reel. Fly-fishing is about passion, observation, nature, adventure, cultural diversity, skill, travel, friendship and any number of other intangibles that add pleasure to the act of casting flies.

Working in the fly-fishing industry as a casting instructor, consultant, guide, writer and photographer has given me the unique opportunity to pursue my passion for fly-fishing at some of the world's premier angling destinations. I would be the first to admit that I have truly been fortunate to be the "someone" tasked with this "tough job."

The result of my life's fly-fishing adventures rests in your hands — my fly-fishing odyssey. This book isn't intended to be another nuts-and-bolts text that rehashes facts and techniques already thoroughly covered by innovators like Lefty Kreh. Nor is it fly-fishing literature in the manner of Roderick Haig-Brown or tongue-in-cheek humor the way only Charlie Waterman can spin it.

My intention is to take you on a quest for some of the world's top freshwater and saltwater game fish, stirring within you the wanderlust and sense of adventure that I believe most fly-fishermen possess. I'll also attempt to answer many of the nagging questions that most traveling fly-fishermen ask themselves at one time or another: Where are the best places to fly-fish? What fly tackle and traveling gear will I need to take to help ensure a successful and enjoyable trip? How do I catch a particular species? Is there anything else to see or do when I'm not fly-fishing?

Another byproduct of my travelogue hopefully will be an increased understanding of the fish you pursue, no matter where you chase them. For instance, many of the nuances of fly-fishing for permit in the Florida Keys may be just as applicable for permit in Belize. Techniques used for trout in Yellowstone National Park can work just as well in Argentina. To tie all this information up into a reference you can use, I've included a section called "The Fishes" at the back of the book. It provides a brief synopsis of the biology of numerous game fish, along with the fly gear needed to catch them at various destinations.

Deserved or not, fly-fishermen have a reputation for being elitists, but money and the enjoyment of fly-fishing at distant locations needn't go hand in hand. Not all of us have the resources to travel to an expensive lodge to catch exotic fish. So for fly-fishers willing to forgo a wine list, gourmet food and fancy quarters, I've included some bargains, along with enough information to make a do-it-yourself trip a real possibility.

Just because a fish hasn't yet attained the legendary status of the trout or permit certainly doesn't make it any less fun or exciting to catch with a fly. My earliest fly-fishing escapades came at a young and tender age when a trip to the creek in the woods down the road from our family home seemed as big an adventure as an Indiana Jones search for lost treasure. In my imagination, the small minnows, hand-sized bluegills and occasional bass that my friends and I caught were as challenging, exciting and extraordinary as some of the bonefish and tarpon that I catch today. That's why I've included pages on some of the common, everyday fish that are available to most fly-fishers.

By the same token, even though the greatest portion of this odyssey takes place in various foreign countries and destinations in the United States, there are also chapters devoted to a few of the wonderful local waters near my home in Geneva, Florida. It's often easy to take for granted the fisheries that may exist in your own backyard. It's the grass-is-greener-on-the-other-side syndrome. However, that's not the case here. My fly-fishing odyssey would not be complete without including those nearby world-class fisheries that have had such an impact on my life.

Let's begin the journey.

CHAPTER 1

RIO PARANÁ:
The Tiger of the Water

Eventually, all things merge into one, and a river runs through it. The river was cut by the world's great flood and runs over rocks from the basement of time. On some of the rocks are timeless raindrops. Under the rocks are the words, and some of the words are theirs. I am haunted by waters.

— Norman Maclean, A River Runs Through It, 1976

I damn near passed up the opportunity to go to Paraguay. The brochures at a local travel agency didn't make it seem too appealing, and that, coupled with the fact that I would be fishing on a muddy river for some obscure species, should have been more than enough to keep me from going. But reason gave way to intuition and curiosity, so on a moment's notice I decided to pack my bags and head for the airport. I wouldn't be sorry.

Several flights later I arrived at the northern Argentine border town of Posadas, a sleepy cluster of street cafes, small shops, gambling establishments and what seemed an inordinate amount of *fumigaciones*, or pest control specialists, most of which featured a picture of a large rat somewhere on the establishment. Maybe it had something to do with the sewage gurgling from manhole grates to form rivulets along the street curbs.

From Posadas, I took a van into Paraguay for a few days of fishing at an obscure lodge upstream from the small settlement of Ayolas on the Parana River. Since several hours of daylight were left, I looked forward to taking in the scenery on the way. But plans can suddenly change in this part of the world.

After a lengthy ordeal at the nearby Paraguayan customs office, where as in many other South American countries bureaucracy is a way of life, it was an hour or so after sunset before I was finally back on the road. My hopes of sightseeing were gone, but even in the darkness I was amazed at the remoteness of the region. In com-

parison with other so-called Third World countries, Paraguay would still be considered undeveloped, and its poverty quickly becomes apparent to any visitor, even one traveling after dark.

Following my late-night arrival and a few hours' sleep at the surprisingly beautiful lodge, my guide, a native Guarani Indian named Javier, greeted me at the boat early the next morning. Still a little bleary-eyed after the arduous trip, I was nonetheless excited by the sights and sounds of the Paraná River. Friendly Guarini hand-lined from dugout canoes, howler monkeys clamored from their perches, thick sub-tropical vegetation crowded the banks and the dark water was full of the remnants of fallen trees. Javier stopped the boat just upstream from one of the biggest snags we had seen, and because of the language barrier, he pointed to the twisted mass and made a casting motion.

As the boat drifted back toward the structure, I made several casts before one apparently got hung up in some submerged branch. I began to wonder if I had packed enough flies for the five days of fishing when suddenly line shot through my hands. Then it went slack.

"Dorado grande," Javier said with a smile and a shrug of his shoulders. I felt like an idiot and wanted to redeem myself immediately. It didn't take long for another chance. This time when the line became taut, I held tight and pulled the rod sharply to the side. Again the line surged toward the deadfall, but heavy rod pressure stopped the powerful run and prevented another break-off. A magnificent golden fish vaulted above the water, and for the next several minutes it intermittently plunged to the depths between wild leaps. Finally, bringing the fish alongside the small boat, I was as mesmerized by the dorado's surreal color as I had been by its strength. It was the strongest freshwater fish for its size that I had ever taken on fly, and one of the most beautiful.

The Paraná's watershed is the second largest in South America, surpassed only by the Amazon River

Paraguay

ASUNCIÓN

Ayolas

Paraná River

Paraná River

The dorado's brilliant golden flanks, black striping and formidable teeth have earned it the nickname "Tiger of the Water."

Basin. Originating at the confluence of the Paranaiba and Rio Grande in southeast Brazil, the upper half of the river forms the boundary between Paraguay and its neighbors, Brazil and Argentina. Its size increases significantly at Resistencia, Argentina, where the river's dark waters merge with those of the Paraguay River. From that point on, the Paraná flows south through Argentina until it converges with the Uruguay River to form the Rio de la Plata estuary in Buenos Aires. The entire distance is approximately 2,000 miles. The river's muddy waters are surprisingly swift with occasional boulder-strewn rapids. Dorado live amongst the huge rocks, as well as in the many submerged dead-falls, along this length.

The dorado is something of an enigma, often confused with other species in the Amazon and Orinoco river basins that are also referred to as "dorado" but are actually piralba. They also are commonly mistaken for the saltwater "dolphin" or "mahimahi" bearing the same nickname. Most of the confusion comes from the fact that "dorado" is Spanish for "golden," the dominant color of all species sharing that nickname.

Various species of true dorado occur naturally in only a few watersheds in the interior of South America. The Paraná River is considered the most important for the largest species of the fish, *Salminus maxillosus* or "dorado grande" as Javier called it. In the Parana system the largest fish can exceed 50 pounds but commonly range between 4 and 20 pounds. Many world-record dorado have been pulled from the stretch of river near Ayolas, where February to November offers the best time to fish.

Dorado have the look and shape of a theoretical subtropical salmon. However, they are powerful fighters, more comparable to saltwater fish of similar size than to the salmonids. Featuring a deep gold mixed with fine black lines and a touch of red at the tail, dorado possess formidable teeth and strong jaws that can immediately sever a monofilament leader and tenaciously hold onto a careless angler's fingers. The combination of strength, coloring and sharp teeth have given rise to the appropriately descriptive nickname "Tiger of the River."

The biggest fish are solitary and prefer the protection submerged structure offers. Such hangouts not only offer protection from the Paraná's strong current, but also act as prime ambush spots. Smaller dorado will sometimes gather in schools, where they can provide almost nonstop action. I often encountered schooling fish around eddies and backflows just off the main current, and in Javier's favorite spot next to a recently completed dam. Although it was a disgusting contrast to the rest of the scenic river, the fly-fishing was outstanding around the retaining walls adjacent to shore.

Not much is known about the feeding habits of dorado. Locals talk about them feeding on a variety of small finfish that inhabit the river, with the eellike knifefish being a favorite bait of the guides and the Guarani Indians trying to put food on the table. The fish never seem to key in on any food source, but they do take advantage of opportunities as they are presented.

Because dorado are indiscriminate feeders and have limited visibility in the murky waters of the Paraná's main channel, bright and fully dressed streamers that push or displace a lot of water worked much better than sparsely tied patterns. I had the most success with large saltwater flies like Blanton's Whistler, my Wobbler and wool-head streamers in sizes 1/0 to 3/0. The jigging action of a Clouser Minnow also worked well. Weed guards help reduce hang-ups, but come prepared to lose a lot of flies to both fish and structure.

You'll appreciate 9-weight tackle for the biggest dorado, but a 7-weight is more fun for smaller schooling fish. Fly lines with a 10- to 30-foot sinking tip will handle most situations. Type III and IV sink rates are both good choices, as are versions with 200- to 325-grain designations.

Leaders should have a short wire shock tippet about 4 or 5 inches long to compensate for the dorado's sharp teeth. Solid trolling wire with a 0.015-inch diameter is a good choice, but I much prefer nylon-coated 19-strand stainless steel wire because its extreme suppleness and small diameter make casting and knot-tying easy.

Regardless of size, dorado are known for short powerful bursts of speed instead of long runs. While a machined reel with a sophisticated drag isn't essential, it can better withstand the rigors of fighting the tough dorado than a lesser model. A lot of backing isn't necessary to play the fish, but it does offer a distinct advantage by increasing the rate of retrieve.

An up-current mend is necessary to give the fly time to sink in the deceptively powerful currents of the Parana. This can be done through the execution of a mend cast or by mending the line the instant it hits the water. Once the fly has sunk, a quick, steady retrieve will draw the most strikes.

Looking back on the wonderful fly-fishing for dorado on the Paraná River, I shudder to think that I almost passed up the opportunity to battle these husky fish amid stained brown currents deep in the heart of South America. That trip fortified my belief that although some fly-fishing trips prove to be more exciting than others, the biggest regret is always that of adventures never taken.

Although Paraguay might be considered an undeveloped nation, that is one of its biggest attractions for the adventurous fly-fisher.

PLANNING A TRIP

Since the Paraná forms part of the Argentina/Paraguay border, anglers have a choice of fishing the river from either country. The Corrientes region of Argentina is known for its excellent dorado fishing and is adjacent to the same part of the river that I fished in Paraguay. The logistics for arranging a trip are probably easier in Argentina because it has more fishing lodges, but traveling through Paraguay perhaps offers a bigger adventure.

Other than mixing with locals and having a few sightseeing opportunities, you'll find few diversions from the Paraná's exciting fly-fishing. Artifacts of pre-Columbian indigenous people are on display in Ayolas, and the ruins of 16th-century Jesuit missions, or reducciones, are scattered nearby. One of the most beautiful natural wonders in the world, Iguazu Falls, awaits those willing to travel a little over 200 miles to the east. There's also a little shopping for local handicrafts, including the intricately woven "nanduti" lace.

CHAPTER 2

THE LAGOONS:
Home Waters

As might be imagined, fishing with the artificial fly can be practiced and enjoyed to the fullest extent where fish are so abundant. I took many different species, both fresh-water and marine, with the artificial fly, in the vicinity of Fort Capron. While they did not run so heavy as those taken with bait, they were quite heavy enough for the fly-rod. For instance, I took crevalle of five pounds, sea-trout of ten pounds, red-fish of five pounds, blue-fish of four pounds, "snooks," or sergeant-fish of six pounds, bone, or lady-fish of two pounds, black bass of eight pounds, and tarpum of ten pounds, in addition to other species of less weight.

— James A. Henshall on Indian River fly-fishing,
from Camping & Cruising in Florida, 1884

The nervous water on the leeward side of the mangrove-lined island looked promising. Silently, I poled the small skiff in for a closer look. Through a semitransparent veil of fog, early light reflected off caudal and dorsal fins that intermittently disturbed the otherwise placid surface. A school of about a half-dozen redfish was foraging lazily through the thick manatee grass that covered the bottom of the shallow estuary.

This morning was typically hot and humid, and the mosquitoes were plentiful. The bloodthirsty creatures whined incessantly while they hovered over exposed parts of my flesh, and I could see my friend Ron Rebeck was having the same problem as he repeatedly swatted bugs with one hand while holding a fly rod in the other.

Distractions aside, the small cove we were fishing was one of our favorite spots for redfish and spotted seatrout. The fish were usually cooperative as well as large, and there was plenty of wildlife to be seen if the fishing action slowed.

After I swung the stern of the boat out of the path of Ron's backcast, he shot the fly just outside the congregation of fish to avoid spooking any that might be on the fringes of the main group. The Li'l

Wobbler landed almost imperceptibly on the water, but it attracted the immediate attention of one of the concealed fish we had anticipated. The water boiled and a V-shaped head wake came in behind the slow-moving fly. Finally, Ron felt tension on the line and lifted the rod to set the hook.

As is often the case, the redfish gave no immediate response; when it turned to swim away, it seemed almost unfazed by the pressure. Then, as if suddenly terrified by the unfamiliar resistance, the red tore across the shallow flat, leaving plumes of mud and a trail of grass in its wake. At the end of its long initial run, Ron began pumping the fish back toward the boat. Intermittently, it would again speed off, but each surge became shorter with the passing minutes. When the redfish finally lay exhausted beneath the starboard gunwale, Ron grabbed it by the tail, removed the fly and returned the fish to the thin layer of water covering the lush sea grasses. The commotion had spooked the other fish we were stalking, but I knew there would be plenty of other opportunities. There always are in The Lagoons.

"The Lagoons" is what people call the greater Indian River Lagoon system on Florida's east-central coast, which includes the interconnected estuaries of Mosquito Lagoon, Banana River and Indian River. Although two of the bodies of water are referred to as "rivers," they are actually true lagoons — isolated bodies of brackish water separated by land from the open sea. Because of this detachment, lagoons are relatively unaffected by tidal fluctuations except in the immediate vicinity of inlets and other openings to the sea. Consequently, water movement is largely the result of wind-driven currents, and sustained winds from the same direction can raise the water level on the windward side of the lagoons to form a sort of "wind tide," or seiche. Water recharge comes from rain, coastal inlets, fresh-water streams, marshes and runoff from small watersheds.

Florida

New Smyrna Beach

Titusville
The Lagoons

Melbourne

From its northern boundary at Ponce de Leon Inlet near Daytona, the Indian River system stretches southward 160 miles to Jupiter Inlet. That's about 40 percent of Florida's east coast, but despite its length the system is only 5 miles wide at its broadest point. The average water depth is approximately 3 to 4 feet, excluding the Intracoastal Waterway.

Climatic differences from north to south combine with the rich estuarine environment of the Indian River Lagoon system to make it one of the country's most diverse and extraordinary ecosystems. Shoreline vegetation is dominated by spartina grass in the north and mangroves in the south. Each of these wetland plants is at the center of a complex food chain, and a variety of sea creatures live in the stems, branches and submerged roots. In the area near Cape Canaveral, spartina and mangroves converge to form a bioregion made up of the flora and fauna from both of the plant-based ecosystems. Coincidentally, the Indian and Banana rivers and Mosquito Lagoon intersect there, too. The unique combination of geography and biology have created an incredible abundance and diversity of plant and animal life.

The sport of saltwater fly-fishing can actually trace some of its roots to the Indian River System. In his book *Camping and Cruising in Florida*, written in 1884, Dr. James Henshall (of *Black Bass* fame) describes using fly-fishing tackle in the 1870s to catch redfish, spotted seatrout, jack crevalle, snook and the first recorded fly-caught tarpon in these waters. All these species remain popular game fish in the lagoon system, but the area is most noted for redfish and seatrout.

Redfish and spotted seatrout are closely related members of the Sciaenadae, or drum, family and therefore have much in common. Each prefers the dense grass flats found throughout most of the lagoon system, but "edges" and "cover" also are favored habitats. In addition to the grassy shallows, hangouts for reds and trout include drop-offs, sandbars, boat docks, oyster beds, current seams and eddies, sandy potholes and

Some of the best fishing within the lagoon system lies in the waters directly adjacent to Kennedy Space Center. Here, a cautious approach is essential to catching gator trout in shallow water.

© BARRY AND CATHY BECK

Casting to sandy potholes while wading the grassy flats is one of the most productive ways to take big seatrout.

than man. Fly-fishers can take advantage of this acute hearing by using flies that produce various sounds and/or vibrations. They should also remember that a quiet approach is essential to avoid frightening these fish.

Spotted Seatrout

Because of their availability, accessibility and willingness to strike artificial lures, spotted seatrout have long been the most popular game fish in Florida. The sheer numbers and large average size of fish in the Indian River Lagoon system have led to the area's reputation as the "seatrout capital of the world," and many world records have been caught in these waters. Years of commercial overharvest eventually decimated trout populations throughout the lagoons, but the 1995 net ban reversed the decline. Today, large "gator" trout — as the locals call fish of more than 6 pounds — are once again taken with regularity from the lagoon system, and occasionally fish of more than 10 pounds are caught. Small "schoolies" can sometimes keep lines tight for hours.

On the flats, nothing is spookier than a large spotted seatrout. And thanks to the fish's reflective sides and natural coloration, their excellent camouflage makes them difficult to see, even at close range. Usually by the time a fly-fisher spots a trout, the fish has long been aware of the angler's presence. That is especially true in the middle of the day when a seatrout is most wary, probably because of its increased vulnerability to predators. From my experience, a gator trout seems more secure and is therefore easier to catch in low-light conditions. The fish actively feed at night, but I prefer to look for them in the late evening and at dawn. In the morning, the best time is between the hour before and two hours after sunrise. The last three hours of daylight are equally good.

Spotted seatrout have upturned mouths and typically attack their prey from below. In the lagoon system, a trout's diet consists almost entirely of penaeid shrimp and small finfish. Whether because of selectivity or opportunity, shrimp make up the majority of the small trout's menu, while finfish are the primary forage base of the larger fish. Flies should be chosen with those feeding characteristics in mind. My fly box for seatrout includes Rattlin' Minnows, popping bugs, Clouser Minnows and, to a lesser degree, bend-backs and keel-hook flies.

Any kid who has ever fished for seatrout knows that the splash and noise made by a popping cork will draw the attention of any seatrout in the area. Hook-and-line commercial trout fishermen also once relied heavily on the loud popping sound of the bobber to help them earn a living. Popping bugs, including cup- and round-faced styles, make a sound almost identical to that of a popping cork, and they're deadly on trout.

One of my favorite ways to catch gator trout in the lagoon system is by blind-casting a 2/0 deer-hair slider while wading a grass flat. I manipulate the slider so it dances and dives across the surface like a wounded baitfish. Sometimes seatrout follow the fly without taking, and sometimes

various structures. Trout and reds usually won't venture far from a nearby plentiful food source, and that is one key to locating them. Depending on seasonal variations, mullet, menhaden, penaeid shrimp and various crabs make up the major part of the forage base for game fish in the lagoons. Because redfish and seatrout share the same prey and habitat, flies and fishing techniques that work on one species usually are effective on the other. As a matter of fact, anglers often catch one species while looking for the other.

One of the most distinguishing characteristics of all members of the drum family is a long lateral line connected to the fish's inner ear via a series of nerves. These allow the fish to detect a wide range of sounds, including vibrations and water movements, at a much lower decibel level

they attack without hooking up. Either way, I keep working the area until the fish either takes the fly, spooks or no longer shows interest.

To effectively cover as much water as possible, I make casts straight ahead and at 45 and 90 degrees on either side of the direction I am wading. After the five casts, I take about five or six steps forward and repeat the procedure. Scouting the flats the day before fishing can pay big dividends. Sandy potholes scattered about the otherwise grassy shallows are prime hangouts for big fish.

Because ambient air temperature almost immediately affects the temperature of shallow water, weather and season greatly influence seatrout movement and feeding habits. During cold snaps, trout will leave the flats to seek the relative warmth of deep water, where they often congregate in large numbers, especially during extended chilly periods. Cold weather decreases the fish's metabolism, which in turn reduces its appetite. The fish will strike only at the slowest-moving flies fished just off the bottom. Combine a sinking line with a neutral density fly to get down where the fish are without hanging up on the bottom. The Eldora area near Canaveral National Seashore in Mosquito Lagoon is famous for its winter trout fishing, and a number of dredge holes and canals throughout the lagoons have good cold-weather fishing as well.

Redfish

Redfish also swim in abundance throughout the Indian River Lagoon System. These fish have strong schooling instincts and tend to gather according to size. They also are creatures of habit, and schools regularly frequent the same area at the same time each day. The average-sized red in the lagoons is about 6 pounds, and "bull" reds weighing more than 20 pounds are relatively common. Several world-record redfish have been caught in these waters; some specimens have exceeded 40 pounds. Nothing in the angling world is more exciting than casting to one of these huge fish feeding quietly on a flat where the water is less than 3 feet deep.

An awareness of wind-driven currents will assist a fly-fisher in finding, spotting and casting to redfish. Reds typically swim into the current to take advantage of foods and scents the moving water carries toward them. Whenever possible, try to take a casting position somewhere upwind and up-current so the fly can be retrieved away from the fish, like some tiny marine animal trying to escape.

In dark waters or when light conditions are poor, I rely on surface disturbances to find fish. V-shaped head wakes, nervous water, scattering bait and protruding tails all indicate that redfish may be in an area. You'll easily distinguish the big wake and straight-lined swimming pattern a redfish makes from the more nervous zigzag swimming action of mullet that frequent the same area. Of course, when the water is clear and light conditions are favorable, the most exciting way to pursue reds in the lagoons is by sight-fishing.

Reds come in to feed on lagoon flats year round, but severe cold or extreme heat drives them into deeper water where temperatures are more stable. The fish can tolerate a wide range of temperatures, but generally prefer water

Indian River, Banana River and Mosquito Lagoon, which together make up the greater Indian River Lagoon system, are famous for their big bull redfish.

FLY GEAR

Rods matched to 7-, 8- or 9-weight lines are well-suited for fly-fishing in the lagoon waters. Light lines and rods are best used for casting relatively small flies to nervous fish on calm days. As wind speed, fish size or fly size increases, so should the size of the rod and line. An 8-weight outfit makes a good all-around choice.

Because conditions in the lagoons change constantly, fly anglers should carry lines of several different densities or sink rates. A floating line can be used in most situations and proves essential for casting over the shallow grass flats, but a mono-core "slime" line or Type III sink-tip line is needed to probe deep holes or the edges of drop-offs.

For spooky fish in skinny waters, leaders 8 to 10 feet long work best, but shorter leaders can be used with sinking lines. Regardless of leader length, tippets should be 0X or heavier to assure adequate turnover of large flies under the frequently windy conditions found in the lagoons. A 20- to 30-pound-test monofilament shock tippet will stand up to the abrasive mouth of the redfish and, to a lesser degree, the seatrout.

As in any type of sight-fishing, polarized sunglasses are a necessity. Like most anglers, I normally use amber-colored lenses for most of my flats fishing, but I also carry along a pair of gray lenses for occasional use in late summer when lagoon sea grasses are especially long and lush. Redfish will sometimes bury themselves in this vegetation, where they can be almost impossible to see. In that situation, I switch to the gray lenses because they actually highlight the blue tip on the redfish's tail when the fish is otherwise camouflaged in the deep grass. Amber lenses block out the blue light — hence the common reference to amber lenses as "blue blockers."

Any selection of shallow-water redfish flies should include Wobblers, deer-hair sliders, bend-backs and Clouser Minnows.

between the mid-60s and mid-80s. Fishing success decreases dramatically outside that range. During the heat of late summer, redfish feed on the flats primarily in the morning and evening when the water is coolest. In winter the fish move into the shallows only after the sun has had time to heat the water. Bear in mind that the water temperature is always higher over dark grassy bottoms than on light-colored sandy bottoms. That's because the dark-colored grass acts as a solar collector that absorbs heat from the sun's rays, which in turn raises the ambient water temperature.

Redfish have the rounded snout and inferior mouth of a bottom feeder and usually prefer to root along the bottom for crustaceans, particularly crabs and shrimp. But they are also opportunistic and will just as readily feed on a variety of finfish. Once they capture their prey, the fish use pharyngeal teeth, or crushers, at the back of the mouth to pulverize the shells, bones or carapaces of their victims. Although some anglers mistakenly believe that reds have poor vision, I have seen fish frightened by the slightest movement or shadow. I've also seen fish turn around in a swoop to take a fly that accidentally landed behind them.

Day in and day out, a Wobbler is my most reliable pattern for redfish, and I use it about 95 percent of the time. I also carry a selection of Clouser Minnows and deer-hair sliders to add a little variety to my fishing. On occasion, I'll use a bendback even though the hookup ratio is slightly less than with standard-gap hooks.

Because of their inferior mouths, redfish have a difficult time positioning themselves to strike topwater flies. I have frequently seen fish continuously twist and turn behind a popper or slider, seemingly to get the proper angle for ingesting it. Furthermore, the fish's head wake may push a high-floating fly off to one side or the other when they try to strike. Sometimes they repeatedly miss a topwater presentation before swimming off in frustration. These problems can be alleviated somewhat by using a hair bug fished in "the film" without floatant and/or a slower stripping speed. Regardless of what changes are made, topwater flies will never be quite as productive as subsurface flies. Nevertheless, they are exciting patterns to use because of the explosive strikes they produce.

Federal Lands

While fly-fishing for redfish and spotted seatrout is excellent throughout much of the Indian River Lagoon system, it takes on world-class proportions in the area surrounding the interconnected federal lands of Merritt Island National Wildlife Refuge, Canaveral National Seashore and Kennedy Space Center, just a few miles east of my home in Geneva. The southern portion of Mosquito Lagoon and the northern extremes of the Banana River and Indian River, which are adjacent to these government properties, offer exceptional sight-fishing opportunities in their clear waters. Gator trout and schools of trophy-sized redfish are abundant here. Fishing is best from March until the end of November, but extended warm weather during the winter can also produce some fantastic shallow-water fly-fishing. Except for the rocket-launching facilities around Kennedy Space Center, the natural beauty of these federally owned lands has been preserved and remains much the same as it was when Dr. Henshall fished here in the 1870s.

The no-motor zone next to Kennedy Space Center at the extreme northern end of the Banana River offers a unique fly-fishing experience for more adventurous anglers. This part of the Banana River is open only to nonmotorized watercraft, such as canoes, kayaks and small sailboats. Because the area receives little fishing pressure, fish are plentiful, aggressive and not easily alarmed. However, fly-fishers should make sure they are in good physical condition before they attempt to paddle a long distance across open water.

Canaveral National Seashore and Merritt Island National Wildlife Refuge have more than 260 miles of earthen dike roads that provide anglers with easy access to prime fishing locations in the southern half of Mosquito Lagoon and the northernmost part of the Indian River. The wading opportunities along these dikes are seemingly limitless, but anglers should exercise caution — the ditches next to these dirt roads have extremely soft, silty bottoms that make them difficult and sometimes dangerous to cross. Fortunately, the flats beyond the ditches have sand or mud bottoms that usually provide relatively firm footing. Wading anglers should also be careful to shuffle their feet while moving to avoid a painful wound from a stingray. Alligators are common to the area as well, and although normally shy and passive toward humans, they should always be treated with respect and given a wide berth.

The greater Indian River Lagoon system offers excellent fly-fishing for other species of fish, including tarpon, snook, jack crevalle and ladyfish. Schools of ladyfish and jack, both of which are aggressive feeders and formidable fighters, are plentiful throughout the lagoons; diving seabirds and showering baitfish often reveal their presence. These fish readily strike fast-moving streamers, and jack crevalle find poppers irresistible.

Tarpon and snook are most common in the warmer southern end. Snook fishing is particularly good near inlets, and baby tarpon up to 35 pounds reside in many coastal rivers and water-management canals and ditches. Just south of the city of Melbourne, the area around Sebastian River can provide plenty of fly-fishing action for both fish. The dike roads of Merritt Island National Wildlife Refuge run adjacent to mosquito-control ditches, many of which contain populations of baby snook and tarpon.

Small watercraft, such as canoes, johnboats and backcountry skiffs, are all ideal for fishing the lagoon flats. To help assure a problem-free trip, anglers should check local marine forecasts and charts. The lagoons develop a nasty chop when it's windy, and submerged bars and shallow water can make navigation difficult in some areas. Numerous professional guides are available for anglers who don't have their own boats and prefer not to wade.

The Indian River Lagoon system offers many unusual contrasts — natural beauty next to space-age technology, peaceful manatees sharing the water with noisy watercraft, pristine wetlands bumping up against waterfront condos, commercial fishermen and catch-and-release fly-fishers using the same boat ramps. Despite these curious dynamics, or perhaps even partly because of them, the lagoons remain one of North America's premier saltwater fishing areas — a mecca for those seeking big redfish and seatrout on the fly.

PLANNING A TRIP

The quaint little coastal town of New Smyrna serves as an ideal base of operations for fly-fishers who want to cast flies to reds and seatrout in lagoon waters surrounding the Kennedy Space Center and Merritt Island National Wildlife Refuge. The tiny community and nearby beautiful beach are situated on the north end of Mosquito Lagoon right next to some of its best fishing. You'll find numerous waterfront hotels and bed-and-breakfasts to choose from, as well as plenty of guides.

I can highly recommend several restaurants. The huge fish sandwiches at Sea Harvest are delicious, yet inexpensive. Riverside Charlie's is a little pricey, but the food is outstanding — don't miss the Sunday brunch. My favorite spot is JB's Fish Camp, where "fun is legal." The place looks a little rustic to first-time visitors, but the local seafood is great.

Several international airports are close by, including those in Orlando, Daytona, Sanford and Melbourne. Rental cars are available at all airport locations.

CHAPTER 3

ISLA MUJERES:
Gateway to Yucatán Fly-Fishing

If you want to live a long and healthy life, learn to be chronically optimistic, hopeful and never leave town without a travel rod.
— *Paul Quinnett,* Darwin's Bass, *1996*

Swells were so high that whenever the 29-foot sport-fisherman lay at the bottom of the trough, we had to look up to see the hookless teaser baits suspended near the top of the wave behind us. Almost a half-hour had passed since we had attracted our last Atlantic sail — one that had been more curious than hungry. Just as I began wondering about how long it might be until our next bite, a group of sails tore through the hookless baits like a pack of marauding wolves. Despite the 20- to 25-knot winds, their dark bodies were clearly visible in the sapphire waters of the Caribbean, but they were too numerous and too quick to count.

Simultaneous cries of "Sail! Sail!" broke the monotonous rumble of the engines as Capt. Anthony Mendillo and crew sprang into action. While Mendillo skillfully maneuvered the boat in the sloppy seas, the mate used one of the trolling outfits to entice the sails within casting distance. One fish in particular had become so obsessed with the bait that it "lit up" in vivid blue hues with its namesake dorsal fin fully extended.

I had positioned myself at the stern with fly rod and reel in hand and about 50 feet of line coiled at my feet. When Mendillo dropped the boat into neutral, I began false casting until the fish was within 25 feet of the stern. The skipper yelled the cue, and the mate yanked the teaser away from the fish. Almost concurrently, I replaced it with my fly.

There was no immediate strike. Instead, the big fish swam impatiently beneath the fly, apparently confused by its lack of motion. I needed to strip the line only once before the sail charged the huge popper and began slashing at it with his spindly beak. Then, after making a quick turn underwater, as if preparing to mount an attack, the sailfish struck and headed for the depths with a mouthful of hackles.

The line immediately came tight in my hand, and I held on to it for a brief moment to set the hook. The fish's initial run was tremendous — running line raced through my left hand as the loose coils cleared the deck. Then the fish was on the reel, and I jabbed the rod sideways several times to further ensure good penetration. In an instant, 30-pound backing was disappearing from the reel while the great fish greyhounded and tail-walked across the horizon in a continuous series of leaps and runs that looked like some furious blue-water ballet.

I bowed the rod to each jump and picked up line at every opportunity, but the power of the sailfish dominated the first half of the battle. Then, after a short stalemate, I could feel the fish begin to tire, and it became increasingly easier to move. Fifteen minutes after the hookup, the exhausted sail lay beside the boat. Anthony grabbed its thrashing bill, removed the hook and slid the fish back over the gunwale for release. Easing into gear, he held the sailfish with its bill facing into the current until he could see its energy and brilliant coloration return. Then it was gone.

In the western Atlantic, sailfish primarily range in blue-water currents from North Carolina to Venezuela. They are members of the billfish family Istiophoridae that also includes marlin and spearfish. Characteristically, all members of this family have an extremely elongated upper jaw that tapers to a rather fine point. However, the huge sail-like dorsal fin is what distinguishes it from other billfish. Although Pacific and Atlantic sails are considered the same fish taxonomically, the average size of a Pacific sailfish runs about twice that of those in the Atlantic. The heaviest specimens in Atlantic waters may grow to 150 pounds, but the average is likely slightly less than 50 pounds. In the Pacific, sailfish average in the 90- to 100-pound range, but can exceed 200 pounds. Because of the disparity in size, the International Game Fish Association

Isla Mujeres

Cancun

Mérida

Mexico

Cozumel

YUCATÁN PENINSULA

© NEAL & LINDA ROGERS

The waters off Isla Mujeres offer many opportunities for one of fly-fishing's most exhilarating moments — sailfish on fly.

places the Atlantic and Pacific fish in two separate categories.

Catching sailfish on fly requires an experienced and accomplished crew who create an environment in which everything works like a finely tuned machine. The procedure is simple in theory, but demanding in execution.

Until a sailfish is raised, all eyes scan the water for fish tailing, basking, feeding, greyhounding or coming in behind one of the hookless teasers. The captain controls the speed and position of the boat, the mate works the fish within casting distance and orchestrates the teasing

procedure, and the flycaster stations himself/herself on the appropriate side of the cockpit.

If two or more baits are trolled, the extra one is promptly reeled in while the mate skillfully manipulates the teaser bait just in front of the sail, pulling it away whenever the fish tries to swallow it. Usually at the direction of the mate, the boat is first put in neutral, and then the teaser gets yanked from the water when the fish is about 30 feet, or a short cast, away. The cast should be timed so that the fly lands immediately after the bait is pulled from the water. Rather than trying to hook the fish as it

SAILS ON FLY

Twelve-weight gear will prove adequate for subduing Yucatán sails. Of course, the heavier gear used for the bigger Pacific fish will certainly bring the smaller Atlantic sails to the boat faster, but it really isn't necessary. Reels should hold about 250 to 300 yards of 30-pound Dacron backing. The tarpon models of most reel manufacturers can double as tools for sailfish. When it comes to recovering line at a rapid rate, the relatively wide diameter a large-arbor reel provides gives a decided advantage, especially when a sail unexpectedly charges toward the boat, leaving yards of slack line in its wake.

A fast-sinking shooting head system is the only line setup I use for sailfishing. Type III and IV sinking shooting heads are the best line choices because they have smaller diameters than slow-sinking and floating lines. The small diameter offers less resistance and therefore less drag in the water than more buoyant lines. The result is a better connection to the fish. Since billfish streamers and poppers are extremely large and heavily dressed, the sinking lines have no significant effect on the buoyancy of the flies.

Fly-fishing for sails requires advanced preparation to prevent last-minute scurrying when the bite is on.

As for running line, I strongly prefer flat monofilament over round monofilament, braided monofilament or level fly line. Braided mono has a rough texture that can severely cut or burn fingers, round monofilament has too much memory for my taste, and in my experience level fly line may separate under extreme stress. On the other hand, flat mono offers high strength, small diameter and almost no memory. Those who insist on a full-length fly line should check out one of the specialty billfish lines.

Big-game or tarpon leaders with a 100-pound shock tippet are standard for this type of fishing. All connections must be meticulously constructed because sailfish will test tackle and knots to their limits, and even the best tackle in the world can't compensate for an inferior knot system.

Rod length is another important factor in fighting sailfish. Long, flexible rods provide poor leverage in fighting fish, and short, stiff rods are difficult to cast. As a compromise, fly rods about 8 feet long makes the best all-around casting and fighting tools for sails.

While some anglers may consider the sailfish's diet when choosing a fly, there's really no need for a "match-the-hatch" mentality here. A hot, teased sailfish doesn't know or care if it's a squid, flying fish, ballyhoo or an old shoe. Whenever possible, I prefer a "match-the-teaser" approach to selecting a fly, choosing an offering that approximates the size and color of the hookless teaser bait to make the switch as easy as possible on less energetic fish. Any basic selection of sailfish flies should include tandem-rigged patterns in white, green/yellow, hot pink and blue/green/white in size 4/0 or 5/0.

swims toward the vessel, I like to cast slightly beyond a sail so that it will take the fly while moving away from the boat, thereby making it easier to set the hook.

The catch is legitimate only if the boat is in neutral and has come to a complete stop when the cast is made. Otherwise the fly is considered to be "trolled" when it lands on the water. To avoid this problem, I always discuss the logistics of the procedure before I go on any offshore charter, emphasizing that I will not cast if the boat is moving forward in the slightest. The best professional crews have always honored my request.

If everything is done right and the sailfish is in a frenzy, the attack will come very shortly after the fly hits the water. Sometimes the strike will be immediate, and on other occasions it will come only after the fly is manipulated. Many times the fish will use its bill to slash at the fly before trying to swallow it. Regardless of when the strike occurs, an angler should not try to set the hook until the fish turns on the fly and the line comes tight. Once the sailfish is hooked, the next concern is to make sure the coiled line clears the deck and goes smoothly through the guides. After the battle is under way, it is important to maintain relentless pressure and to retrieve line at every opportunity to tire the fish as quickly as possible. If the angler takes time to rest, the fish also has time to renew its energy. To keep the hook from dislodging and to reduce the chances of a tippet breaking, be prepared to bow the rod whenever the fish jumps.

Although the blue water of the Caribbean Sea at the eastern tip of the Yucatán Peninsula is recognized as one of the premier destinations in the world to catch Atlantic sailfish, the area hasn't really caught on with fly-fishers to the same degree that other sailfish hot spots have. That's partly because only a few experienced fly-fishing charter services are sprinkled around Cancun, Cozumel and Isla Mujeres.

Yet the situation is improving. In fact, I'd have to say that Mendillo ranks as one of the best offshore fly-fishing guides I've ever fished with anywhere. Both his 29-foot *Keen M* and equally nice 36-foot *Lilly M* are equipped with first-class fly tackle for those who need it. Mendillo is thoroughly familiar with the intricacies of offshore fly-fishing, and I can attest to his uncanny ability to raise fish under even the toughest conditions. The fact that he's a genuinely nice guy adds to the pleasurable experience.

His base of operations is the quaint island at the tip of the Yucatán known as Isla Mujeras. Early Mayans used the island as a sanctuary from which they could worship Ixchel, the goddess of fertility, medicine, reason and the moon. Upon landing there in 1517, Francisco Hernandez de Cordova, the famous Spanish conquistador, discovered a number of statues of the female idol, her daughters and daughters-in-law at the

A prominent statue in the island's quaint village acknowledges Isla Mujeres' long fishing history.

temple on the island's southernmost tip. Finding no male idols, Cordova dubbed the island Isla Mujeres, or "island of women." Over the next 300 years, Isla Mujeres remained uninhabited except when, in a bit of irony, pirates and fishermen left their women on the island during periodic trips to the sea.

These days, many of this island's visitors could be said to worship the sailfish, given the area's annual spring run that draws fishermen and boats from all over the U.S. and abroad. During peak season here, I've seen more than 30 sails in the teasers, frequently coming in groups of five or more. On one exceptionally good trip, Mendillo released 70 fish — yes, 70 — while fishing with anglers who preferred trolling. Consequently, fly-fishers can expect plenty of exciting action, too.

Although casting flies to teased sailfish may not represent the purest form of fly-fishing, you'll be hard-pressed to find anything in the angling world more exhilarating to watch — unstoppable high-speed runs, magnificent vaulting leaps and tail walks that seem to defy the laws of gravity. For many, the sailfish represents one of fly-fishing's greatest prizes, and there are few better places to catch that prize than the dark-cerulean sea currents of the Yucatán.

PLANNING A TRIP

Isla Mujeres lies only a short cab ride and a half-hour trip by water taxi, or "fast boat" as the locals call it, from the Cancun airport, but it's eons away in development and pace of living. Visitors to the island can enjoy diving on nearby reefs, bargain hunting at local shops, exploring Mayan ruins, sunbathing on sandy beaches or just kicking back with some homemade ice cream and mingling with the locals at the charming town square. I love the place and its friendly people — a welcome contrast to fast-paced Cancun.

Stay at Hotel Cabañas Maria del Mar, a surprisingly moderate-priced beachfront hotel owned by Capt. Anthony Mendillo's in-laws. The beautiful resort's amenities include a swimming pool, seaside bar and an excellent restaurant.

Why not combine fly-fishing for sailfish with a trip to the flats? Ascension Bay's world-class fly-fishing for tarpon, permit and bonefish is only a few hours' drive south of Cancun. See Chapter 17 — "Ascension Bay: Heavenly Fly-Fishing."

31

CHAPTER 4

PATAGONIA:
Trout of the Andes

About halfway down the run, in water silvery with sunlight, a 3-pound brown trout took the fly in a swirl of gold against silver. The color and light of the fish and the place were so vivid and strong that they have remained alive with me, subject to recall whenever I wish.
— Roderick L. Haig-Brown, "River of the Pampas"
in Fisherman's Winter, 1954

The large and radiantly white glaciers of the high Andes contrasted beautifully with the conifer forest and cloudless blue sky. Although the scenery spoke volumes, the wooden oars grating against their locks was the only sound that could be heard above the gurgling riffles of the swiftly flowing Futaleufu River. Martin O'Farrell, my Argentine guide, rowed the inflatable raft to the edge of a gravel bar that dropped into a pool. I stepped from our boat into the cold river and began casting a Prince nymph where various currents converged into a long, deep run.

The first cast did not meet success, but the line momentarily hesitated at the end of the second drift, and I instinctively raised the rod to a jarring strike. A rainbow trout shot into the air, its sides deeply saturated with the prismatic colors of its namesake. I followed the fish's run downriver for several minutes until it came thrashing to the surface. Kneeling in the shallows, I slipped a net under the tired rainbow and paused to admire the wonderful fish. It was one of those brief reflective moments that heighten the senses. The warm sun seemed comforting, the cold current was exhilarating, the river appeared to be brighter, the mountains more majestic, and the beautiful rainbow that had provided me with so much pleasure felt like the very essence of life as it undulated slowly from my hands.

The eggs and young of rainbow, brown and brook trout were introduced into many of Argentina's lakes and streams early in the 20th century, around 1904. Ideal weather, cold and highly oxygenated waters and plentiful food have created a large and healthy population of salmonids, particularly in the south and the southwest. Argentina has ensured the future of these fisheries through good management principles, including the prohibition of baitfishing in many areas. A number of the best trout streams and lakes are included in and protected by the country's excellent national park system.

The Patagonia region, near the southwestern town of Esquel, offers some of the country's best and most varied fly-fishing for rainbow, brown and brook trout. Although the occasional trophy-sized trout is taken from one of the area's numerous lakes, spring creeks, dam tailwaters and freestone streams, fat fish in the 2- to 4-pound range are more the norm. Compared with the more famous rivers of Junin de los Andes to the north, the waters near Esquel receive far less fishing pressure, so a fly-fisher can easily go for days without seeing another angler. Furthermore, regardless of which body of water you fish, the majestic Andes Mountains provide a spectacular backdrop that makes superb fishing even more enjoyable.

Some of the region's most beautiful, and productive, waters are located within the magnificent Los Alerces National Park, named after a large native conifer. The park has 12 major lakes as well as scores of streams and rivers from which to choose. Among the most important lakes are Rivadavia, Futalaufquen, Krugger, Menendez and Verde. Major rivers that offer some of the best fishing include Arrayanes, Rivadavia, Menendez, Frey Desaguadero and Carrileufu. The smaller streams offer outstanding fishing as well, and all waters have strictly enforced catch-and-release regulations. A fly-fisher can reach a lot of wadeable water via the park's system of trails and well-maintained gravel roads, but a float trip is the most productive way to fish many of the rivers. It also affords the best opportunity to view the beautifully unspoiled and varied terrain of Los Alerces.

BUENOS AIRES

Argentina

Zapala

Los Alerces
National Park

Esquel

Patagonia

The Rivadavia River serves as a prime example of the park's high-quality fishing. It flows slowly at the base of jagged peaks and rocky moraines that contain the Rivadavia along its short 4-mile run. The deep-cut banks, gin-clear water, submerged logs, tree-lined shore, gravel bars and dark pools of this freestone stream provide excellent habitat for healthy populations of rainbow and brown trout. Fish average 2 pounds, but 5-pounders are not at all uncommon.

My first glimpse of the Carraleufu reminded me somewhat of tropical salt flats — transparent water that took on an azure blue in the river's deep bends, holes and pockets. The coloration of the fish proved equally amazing. The brown trout had a bright golden glow, while the 'bows were tinted vividly in red, green and silver. The clear water made for some tough fishing, and the lightest tippets were often necessary for consistent hookups. But the Carraleufu's fish frequently exceeded 20 inches and tested wispy leaders to the fullest extent.

The immediate area outside the park also has a number of excellent fishing spots, but the Futaleufu is one of the more outstanding. Most of the waters of Los Alerces National Park lie within the watershed of this extraordinary river. The Futaleufu is a large, wide and swift-flowing river that runs through Chile before emptying into the Pacific Ocean. At first glance, it reminds you of the Yellowstone River. Some of its rainbow and brown trout will weigh more than 10 pounds, although the average size is 2 to 4 pounds. The river is wadeable, but access is limited

ANDES ACCESSORIES

Since Argentina is in the Southern Hemisphere, its seasonal calendar is opposite that of the United States. Though the Patagonia area is fishable from November through mid-April, the best time is between January and April when the rivers are no longer adversely affected by melting snow.

During the peak fishing period, temperature and weather can vary significantly from day to day. While most summer days in Argentina are warm and sunny, the weather can be cool and rainy. Temperatures may range from the 50s to the mid-80s during the day. Take a variety of clothing to handle daily climatic fluctuations. Lightweight chest waders will prove comfortable enough for most lakes and rivers, but a layer of warm pile clothing can come in handy in the coldest waters or when the temperature drops.

Those equipped to fish the American West will feel right at home in this area of the Patagonia. Four-, 5- and 6-weight outfits are ideally suited to Argentine trout streams. A 4-weight will suffice on slow-moving and still waters, while a 6-weight will help fly-fishers cast heavily weighted streamers and land big fish in large, swift-flowing rivers. As an all-around outfit, the 5-weight represents a good choice.

To fish productively under a variety of conditions, carry both floating and sink-tip lines. Of course, you'll use a floating line for drifting dry flies, and it can also be used for subsurface fishing in slow water. In strong currents and where the water runs deep, however, a sink-tip line offers a distinct advantage for nymphs and streamers. Anglers fishing mountain lakes should also consider bringing along a sinking line. Use leaders approximately 10 feet long for dry-fly fishing, shorter leaders on sinking and sink-tip lines to keep a nymph or streamer down where it belongs.

A wide variety of common fly patterns will draw strikes from the aggressive trout of the Andes. Any assortment of dry flies should have sizes 12 through 16 Adams, Royal Wulffs, Humpies, Elk Hair Caddis and a few terrestrial patterns, including hoppers, crickets and ants. Sizes 10 to 14 Girdle Bugs and Woolly Worms, along with Hare's Ear, Zug Bug and Prince nymphs, are among the most productive subsurface patterns. Effective streamers include olive, brown and black Woolly Buggers and Matukas, as well as Muddler Minows in sizes 4 to 8. According to guide Martin O'Farrell, most Argentine waters experience few notable insect hatches, and at best they occur sporadically. The most productive presentation is often near the bottom with streamers and nymphs.

A large part of the diet of Patagonian trout consists of pancora crabs, olive-colored crustaceans that inhabit the cold watersheds of the Andes. To imitate these small and plentiful crustaceans, locals use a variety of patterns from about 3/4 inch to 3 1/2 inches long. A few of the imitations I've seen resemble a Wooly Bugger with an olive back and a light-green underbelly. Every angler prospecting for trout in the region's rivers should have a few pancora patterns in the fly box.

since a good portion of it is surrounded by large, private *estancias*. Therefore, you'll need a small boat to take full advantage of the Futaleufu's prime fishing.

The now-famous Arroyo Pescado is a beautiful spring creek that originates in the semiarid grasslands, or *pampas*, a few miles northeast of Esquel. This quiet, pastoral stream is a fly-fishing-only, catch-and-release fishery on private land, and anglers must have the owner's permission to enter. Arroyo Pescado contains plenty of eager rainbows, and fly-fishers can expect to catch 20-plus fish per day. The fat rainbows there average 14 to 16 inches in length, and some specimens grow to 5 pounds or more, though thick aquatic vegetation makes it difficult to land these larger fish. Arroyo Pescado is known not only for great fishing, but also because the infamous outlaw Butch Cassidy is said to have killed a local citizen whose marked grave rests along the creek's bank.

There's a lot more to the Patagonia region than the excellent trout fishing and beautiful mountain scenery. Visiting anglers will want to sample the incomparably delicious pastries and breads freshly prepared in clay ovens at local bakeries. Argentina's wines are also outstanding, and its beef is renowned for its flavor. Try to eat at a local barbecue that serves beef, mutton and goat prepared over an open-pit fire. Visitors may be asked to sample yerba maté, a tealike brew that is often shared by friends

drinking from a communal cup with strawlike utensils.

Esquel and the surrounding countryside seem almost to have been lost in a wonderful time warp. It is a remote and unspoiled region without many of the complications of more hectic settings. The people are amaz-ingly warm and friendly, the pace is slow and the small, quiet villages are charming without being backward. In this part of Patagonia, ox-drawn carts and gauchos on horseback share the road with bike riders and motor vehicles — a sort of South American Mayberry.

I also recommend a trip into nearby Chile since it's only a short drive from Esquel. Its chocolate alone is worth the drive, and the fishing is every bit the equivalent of that in Argentina. However, a word of warning: The two countries are not friendly with each other, and there have been occasional disputes over borderlines. As a result, crossing from one country into another can turn into an unpleasant experience. Normally a detailed inventory (that includes serial numbers) of personal items is required for both entry and departure. The soldiers that control the border stations are often unfriendly and impatient. In an episode that reminded me of Roderick Haig-Brown's *Fisherman's Winter*, I was taking shots of a picturesque station in the mountains when I was admonished with a stern, "No, no, señor." An armed soldier wanted my expensive camera and lens, and without some quick talking from my guide I'm sure both would have been confiscated. Apparently things haven't changed much since Haig-Brown's visit almost 40 years ago.

That incident is no indication of how the Argentines, or Chileans for that matter, treat their visitors. To the contrary, it is their very hospitality and warmth that help make this part of the world so inviting. Sometimes it's hard to decide which is more enjoyable — the fantastic fishing, beautiful scenery, superb foods or the friendly people.

Some excellent fly-fishing is available alongside lightly traveled gravel roads. Many of these Patagonia streams are full of eager trout as well as some trophy-sized fish.

PLANNING A TRIP

Rustic lodges and primitive campsites in Los Alerces National Park, as well as the area's other parks, are available to fly-fishers who prefer a self-directed trip, but the most efficient way to fish is with a properly outfitted and knowledgeable guide. They will provide the rafts and boats necessary to reach many of the best waters and the equipment needed for a successful trip.

In the past, such services have been limited in this part of the Patagonia, but the number of guides and lodges is rapidly increasing as the region continues to gain popularity. One of the finest and most hospitable outfitters I have used is O'Farrell Safaris and its Trevellin Lodge. In addition to overseeing a staff of knowledgeable fly-fishing guides, Martin O'Farrell provides ground transportation, fishing licenses and lodging, and offers exquisite regional dishes and wines on each trip. His chef brother displays his culinary expertise on each day's menu.

Traveling from outside Argentina to Patagonia usually requires an overnight stay in Buenos Aires, a city with a cosmopolitan, almost European feel to it. A trip down Avenida de Mayo or Avenida Nueve de Julio reveals much of the flavor of Buenos Aires and immediately brings to mind the political uprisings that have played such a large role in the country's history. Sidewalk cafes, exceptional restaurants, historic areas, world-class soccer, beautiful architecture, shopping and an art colony are only some of the attractions here. Visitors may also want to stop at one of the local clubs to watch professional dancers tango.

CHAPTER 5

BIMINI:
Island in the Stream

The water of the Stream was usually a dark blue when you looked out at it when there was no wind. But when you walked out into it there was just the green light of the water over that floury white sand and you could see the shadow of any big fish before he could ever come in close to the beach. Across the flats the sand was bone white under the blue sky and the small high clouds that were traveling with the wind made dark moving patches on the green water.

— *Ernest Hemingway,* Islands in the Stream, *1970*

Bimini has a rich angling history, and its waters remain legendary, thanks in large part to Hemingway, Zane Grey and many other notable anglers/authors who have publicized the quality fishery around this westernmost island in the Bahamas. While most of Bimini's notoriety comes from its outstanding blue-water fishery, the shallow water in the backcountry offers angling opportunities that are equally good.

One of the primary reasons for the high-quality and varied fishing is Bimini's proximity to rich, productive water. The deep-blue current of the Gulf Stream skirts the island's western shore, while broad, sandy flats cover the eastern side. In this ideal geographic location, fly-fishers can pursue a variety of marine game fish in both shallow and deep water. Consequently, deciding where to fish is usually a pleasant dilemma, but neither choice is disappointing.

The Flats

Because bonefish are one of my favorite fly-fishing targets, I usually opt for a trip to the shallows on Bimini's east side. These flats are a mixture of mangrove islands, gin-clear water and bright, sandy bottom with occasional patches of turtle grass — the quintessential habitat for bonefish. Nevertheless, anglers often overlook Bimini as a prime destination to catch the gray ghost. That's probably because the small island doesn't have the vast flats

found in some other locales, such as Andros in the Bahamas and Ascension Bay on Mexico's Yucatán Peninsula.

What Bimini lacks in area, however, it more than makes up for in the quality of the fishery, particularly when it comes to hefty bonefish. Several world records have come from the island's flats, including Jim Orthwein's 15-pounder, the largest recorded bone taken with a fly. That catch was no fluke, either. Over years of regular visits to Bimini, Orthwein has used his fly rod to consistently catch bonefish weighing in excess of 12 pounds.

Nothing makes my heart pound as hard as approaching one of these big, solitary bonefish feeding in quiet, shallow water. No other fishing situation presents more of a challenge, and in Bimini there's plenty of challenge to go around. I have regularly seen fish over 10 pounds in water barely deep enough to cover their backs. These tailing bonefish are normally so focused on their prey that they won't notice a fly unless it is immediately in front of them — and even that doesn't always draw their interest. I've found that working the fly after the fish has stopped tailing will often get its attention; the fly is much more likely to be seen when the bone is no longer preoccupied with food.

While one of Bimini's legendary 15-pounders has yet to come my way, I've found plenty of fish over 8 pounds to cast to and have landed one that weighed close to 12. The largest bones are often solitary and extremely difficult to approach. The fish may spook seemingly for no reason at all; however, boat noise, shadows, abrupt movements and sloppy casts are sure to send these giant bonefish streaking off the flats like speeding torpedoes.

Bimini's smaller bonefish can provide plenty of excitement, too. Fish weighing less than 4 pounds often gather in vast schools on the flats. I've seen the enormous plumes of mud a large gathering of these smaller fish stir up as they root along the bottom. They are usually aggressive feeders and can provide steady action as

Florida

Miami

Bimini

The gin-clear waters of Bimini's backcountry are teeming with bonefish. While the flats hold plenty of large fish, it also is home to vast schools of smaller specimens.

long as they aren't frightened. I like to carry a 5- or 6-weight rod along to use when I locate a school of bantam mudders, but it's a good idea to keep a 7- or 8-weight handy in case small groups of bigger fish show up. Since bonefish ordinarily move into the tidal flow, a cast to the up-current side of the mud will more often than not produce a strike. The rear portion of the mud generally produces fewer strikes unless the fish are milling around an area.

I've found any number of flies to be effective for Bimini's bonefish, including Crazy Charlies, Clouser Minnows and other sparsely dressed inverted patterns. I generally choose colors that closely match the bottom of the flats that I'm fishing. While I strongly favor olive-colored patterns for these waters, brown, tan, pink and off-white flies also work well. Most fly-fishers prefer patterns tied on hook sizes 4 through 8, but I have used size 2 hooks with a great deal of success. Short, quick strips that skip

Chumming nearby reefs and wrecks can produce a variety of fish including cero mackerel and sharks (bottom). Monster bluefin tuna, like this one caught trolling (far right), have earned Bimini its reputation for big-game fishing.

the fly along the bottom will usually draw a bonefish's attention.

Several competent guides work out of the Bimini Big Game Fishing Club. I've fished with many of them, and they have always been able to locate fish — even under less-than-favorable conditions. One of my most interesting trips was with guide Ansil Saunders. His repartee about the Healing Hole, where Martin Luther King Jr. wrote his "I have a dream" speech, as well as his knowledge of other island history, adds a great deal to any trip to the flats. He's also a boatbuilder of some renown, and his beautifully functional skiff is testimony to his skill.

Offshore

Since a large portion of Bimini's angling reputation comes from its extraordinary oceanic fishery, no fly-fishing trip is complete without testing the open waters of the Atlantic that are only minutes from the dock. There, marlin, sharks, sailfish, jack, tuna, dolphin, snapper and mackerel represent just a few of the species of fish that may be encountered in the nearby Gulf Stream and reef areas.

While several offshore charter boats are available in Bimini, I prefer chartering a boat in Miami and taking the short 50-mile trip across the Gulf Stream — weather permitting, of course. Why? First, the relatively calm seas during the warm months, when I prefer to venture offshore, make the crossing interesting and relaxing. Secondly, my experience in locating charter boats that specialize in offshore fly-fishing has been better in Florida than in Bimini.

One of my most memorable forays into Bimini's offshore waters

occurred when two friends and I set course for the island with Capt. Bouncer Smith. Before our predawn departure from Miami, we had filled the livewells with pilchards netted and hooked around a local pier. After a two-hour cruise across the calm summer seas of the Gulf Stream, Bouncer used his GPS to locate some wrecks around the reefs

directly adjacent to Bimini's shoreline. His combination of ground chum and live pilchards instantly drew a wide variety of large and small fish within casting range of our flies. The clear waters of the reef looked like a magnificent aquarium filled with innumerable fish species, and stayed that way throughout most of the day. During our stay, we landed and released sharks that topped 150 pounds, giant amberjack, barracuda, an assortment of snapper, hard-fighting jacks and even a few small king mackerel.

Just past Bimini's reefs, pelagic species roam the cobalt depths, where I once watched in awe as a bluefin tuna in the 600-pound range ripped through the teaser baits being trolled behind our boat. The giant fish was far beyond the capabilities of the fly tackle we were using, but it was a magnificent sight to watch all the same. The awesome incident further emphasized the dichotomy that exists in the very short distance between Bimini's bonefish flats and its plunging abyss.

A fly-fisher could conceivably carry a small arsenal of outfits to fish for the wide variety of species around Bimini's reefs, wrecks and offshore waters. However, as a guideline, a 10- and 12-weight rod matched to reels that respectively hold 200 and 300 yards of 30-pound backing will handle most situations. The addition of an 8- or 9-weight will handle small snappers and jacks.

In almost all instances, I would recommend using Type IV sinking shooting heads attached to a flat monofilament running line such as Cortland Cobra. The small diameter of a sinking shooting head system offers less drag resistance in the water than a comparatively large-diameter floating fly line. That's especially important with the largest and fastest offshore species, where close, direct contact with the fish can bring significantly more landings. Fly-fishers will also need to carry an ample supply of big-game-style leaders with both wire and heavy monofilament shock tippets.

The Compleat Angler, a former Hemingway hangout, is one of many places to visit on the island at the end of a day's fly-fishing.

Fly patterns and sizes should be as diverse as the many varieties of game fish. Clouser Minnows, Lefty's Deceivers, tandem-hook billfish flies and large, fully dressed hair bugs are staples for Bimini's deepwater scene. Choose flies tied in white, yellow, blue, chartreuse, hot pink and combinations thereof. I'd also recommend taking along some chum flies in case the captain and crew decide to put out a chum line.

The island of Bimini has long established itself as one of the premier fishing destinations in the world. With anglers flocking to newly discovered hot spots, it's often easy to overlook old favorites. That's unfortunate, because quite often the best fishing is right in our own backyard.

PLANNING A TRIP

Because of its proximity to Florida, Bimini is an attractive and easy-to-get-to foreign destination for many U.S. citizens. Chalk's International Airline maintains a fleet of reliable Mallard seaplanes that make regularly scheduled flights from Miami and Fort Lauderdale. Chalk's also offers packages that include accommodations and air transportation.

Chartering a boat in Florida for the cruise to Bimini is another viable and adventurous alternative. Capt. Bouncer Smith is thoroughly familiar with island waters, and I am confident he can find fish. Regardless of the mode of transportation used, a passport or birth certificate is needed to enter Bahamian waters.

Arrangements for guides and lodging in Bimini can be made through the Bimini Big Game Fishing Club, a full-service resort that caters especially to anglers. There is no shortage of good restaurants on the island, which include the one at the Big Game Club. I highly recommend the Bimini Bay at the northern tip of the island for its excellent fare, as well as the outstanding ocean view, fine selection of Cuban cigars and tasteful decor. If you've never tried the island's uniquely delicious Bimini Bread, ask for it at any restaurant.

CHAPTER 6

WELAKA:
River of Lakes

The last time I walked in the swamp
I sat upon a cypress stump.
I listened close
And heard the ghost
Of Osceola cry.
Blow, blow, Seminole wind.
Blow like you're never gonna blow again.
I'm callin' to ya like a long lost friend
'Cause I know who you are.
And blow, blow from the Okeechobee
All the way up to Micanopy.
Blow 'cross the home of the Seminoles,
The alligators, and the gar.

— *John Anderson, "Seminole Wind"*
from the album Seminole Wind, *1992*

A sporadic succession of startled alligators slid from the banks as I maneuvered the small johnboat through an intricate maze of never-ending bends, sloughs and channels that connect one lake to another in the remote upper portion of Florida's St. Johns River. An extended drought had reduced the river to its lowest level in recent memory, and the gators were gathered around what little water was left. Each of the few remaining deep pools not only attracted several of the prehistoric reptiles, but also served as a sanctuary for the huge population of largemouth bass isolated from the cover of the thick, natural shoreline vegetation so abundant when the river is high.

Just before coming to one of these large pools, I brought the aluminum skiff off plane and killed the engine to avoid spooking the nearby bass. My friend Kevin Oglesby and I slid over the side of the boat and pulled it up on the sandy bank, grabbed our rods and followed the river's edge a short dis-

tance along a prominent mud bank that leads to the deep hole. Having fished this same spot for many years during low-water conditions, we eagerly anticipated the numbers of hungry bass that would find our flies irresistible. Still, neither of us was prepared for the feeding frenzy we witnessed as we looked out over the water. Schools of small minnows fearfully flew from the water, chased by bands of marauding largemouth, stripers and hybrid sunshine bass. The entire surface was boiling with activity.

In the two hours before sunset, most of our casts were met by largemouth, but sometimes a striper or sunshine would strike one of our offerings. The majority of all the fish, no matter what species, weighed between 2 and 4 pounds but several were larger, and one largemouth even topped 10 pounds. We occasionally paused from fishing to revel in the moment and wonder at the pandemonium.

The scene continued until the sun had long settled and the mosquitoes began to make us uncomfortable. Then I fired up the small outboard and throttled the boat through the puzzled darkness as swarms of tiny "chizzywinks" — as old Floridians call blind mosquitoes — stung our faces on the way to the dock.

The beginning of hurricane season was still over a month away. Then the almost daily ritual of afternoon showers would eventually raise the narrow band of water over its banks to spread for miles across the vast floodplain. The lush aquatic vegetation would return, and once again the bass would swim amid the thick mats of floating hydrilla, canopies of water lilies, submerged logs, emergent plants and other structure that make this a world-class bass fishery. Until that time, Kevin and I would fill our late afternoons with curious alligators and jumping bass.

The St. Johns is one of the few large rivers in North America whose current runs from south to north. The river originates in the sawgrass swamps and wetlands of Indian River County a few miles west of Vero Beach in southeast Florida.

Jacksonville

Florida   St. Johns River

Sanford
Orlando

The upper
St. Johns River
offers some of the
finest fly-fishing for
largemouth bass in
the world.

There it begins as a miles-wide shallow sheet of water that moves almost imperceptibly toward the north, much like the broad flow of fresh water that forms the Everglades in the south.

The Seminoles called it "Welaka," which translates into "river of lakes," a description that is readily apparent to those who know the river or refer to a map. The channel begins to form a little south of Lake Hell 'n Blazes, the first of many lakes created and connected by the St. Johns as it meanders slowly along a 310-mile course to its confluence with the Atlantic Ocean near Jacksonville. In succession, major lakes include Sawgrass, Washington, Winder, Poinsett, Halfway, Cone, Ruth, Clark, Loughman, Puzzle, Harney, Mullet, Mud, Thornhill, Jessup, Monroe, Beresford, Woodruff, Dexter and George

In his journal of 1791, pioneering naturalist William Bartram describes some of his companions using a flylike "Florida Bob" to catch largemouth bass (he referred to them as "green trout") on the St. Johns. Bartram claims that some of the specimens "frequently weigh 15, 20 and 30 pounds." While his book is an interesting account of Florida flora and fauna in the later half of the 18th century, it is also prone to great exaggeration at times. Nevertheless, the fishing must have been fantastic.

Although the river offers outstanding fly-fishing throughout its length, my favorite stretch is the upper section from Lake Monroe, near the

Areas with floating leaf plants serve as prime habitat for largemouth and a host of other unique wildlife (inset), but such habitat requires weedless flies to avoid hang-ups.

SIMPLE PLEASURES

Simplicity — that's what appeals to me most about fly-fishing for bass. It is to the world of fly-fishing what minimalism is to art. Part of the beauty of the sport is in its basic unpretentiousness. There's no need for lots of fancy equipment. Besides a rod and reel, all I carry in my tackle bag is a fly box filled with poppers and streamers, along with some spools of leader material and a hook sharpener.

I've seen anglers use everything from a 2- to a 10-weight on the river system. The lighter outfits are fun when catching small bass in relatively weed-free water such as creek mouths, but they don't have the backbone to take medium or large Florida bass in thick cover. Fly-fishers who use heavy gear, 9- and 10-weights, are usually casting huge flies for trophy bass in dense vegetation. Nevertheless, such stout tackle is overkill. I've taken several fish over the years that pushed 10 pounds and have never needed anything heavier than an 8-weight. Besides, the stronger rods aren't much fun on the average-sized St. Johns largemouth that you'll encounter 99.9 percent of the time. For all-around bass fishing on the river, 6- through 8-weight tackle is a good choice. My favorite rod is a 7-weight because it casts most bass flies with relative ease and is strong enough to play big bass in cover without being too overpowering on small ones. You'll want stout leaders, 0X and larger, to turn over large flies and to pull fish out of dense plant growth. Since vegetation accumulates around the knots of hand-tied leaders, stick with knotless ones.

Casting for bass presents its own problems. If you aren't occasionally getting hung up, then your casts probably aren't getting close enough to the cover or structure that bass prefer. With a good helmsman manning the trolling motor or oars and keeping the boat a consistent distance from shore, I can make my casts the same length each time and drop the fly precisely where I want it. To do this, I first must make a cast that lands within a few inches of the bank. Then I step on the line immediately at my feet so that after I strip in the line, the next cast will shoot exactly the same distance as the previous one.

Casting into and along the edges of aquatic vegetation will draw the most strikes from bass.

small town of Sanford, to its headwaters around Lake Hell 'n Blazes. The St. Johns is a much more intimate and pristine river there than in the lower reaches where boat traffic and development have an increasingly negative influence on the character of the riverine environment. In contrast, the upper one-third of the river slowly meanders through a mixture of broad prairie, lush subtropical vegetation, spongy marshes and high hammocks of pine, moss-draped oaks and tall palms. Thick aquatic vegetation is abundant here, and it provides the perfect habitat for large

numbers of fat, healthy bass for which the river has become famous. To consistently catch largemouth on the St. Johns year round, you must first identify various types of productive habitat.

Largemouth Bass Habitat

Bodies of water are classified according to the level of nutrients — phosphates and nitrates — they contain. Lakes, ponds and rivers that are nutrient-poor are called "oligotrophic," while waters that are rich

The St. Johns is known for its big bass, as well as for large numbers of surface-thrashing schoolies.

hardiest of non-game-fish species such as carp and other "rough" fish. Eutrophic water with an overabundance of nutrients has a green, "pea-soup" appearance, and large algae mats may be present.

Eutrophication is a natural aging process that continuously occurs in all bodies of water, both eutrophic and oligotrophic, as nutrients collect in ever-increasing amounts. Normally an oligotrophic body of water evolves into a eutrophic one over thousands of years, but the process can be astonishingly accelerated when fertilizers, sewage, livestock wastes, phosphate detergents, industrial waste and other pollutants are added. Such hypereutrophic, or weed-choked, bodies of water may eventually become "dead," like Lake Apopka, the second largest lake in Florida. Decades of runoff containing fertilizers and animal waste from adjacent farms and ranches has completely destroyed the lake once considered the best bass fishery in the state, and possibly the world. Pollutants haven't yet had the same devastating effects on the St. Johns, largely because the river's current is constantly flushing these contaminants into the sea, which creates a whole new set of problems. But I digress.

in nutrients are designated as "eutrophic." In general, the more nutrients a body of water contains, the more aquatic plant and animal life it supports.

Oligotrophic waters have a low nutrient level, usually the result of cold, clear water, sparse plankton, few rooted plants and, characteristically, a deep basin with a sand or gravel bottom. Members of the trout family are commonly associated with nutrient-poor water, though largemouth bass can survive and even thrive there as well.

However, ideal habitat for largemouth bass is eutrophic; more and bigger bass are caught in these easily identified waters. Besides being rich in nutrients, eutrophic waters are generally shallow basins with muddy bottoms, abundant plankton, plentiful rooted vegetation and warm, somewhat turbid water — coincidentally a perfect description of the St. Johns watershed. At times, good bass habitat is akin to a salad bowl.

Healthy eutrophic waters that are prime environments for bass should not be confused with the oxygen-depleted quagmires overgrown with blue-green algae that contain excessive nutrients and support only the

Regardless of whether water is eutrophic or oligotrophic, largemouth bass regularly reside near some type of cover, structure, food source or water feature. "Cover," in this context, is a catchword used to describe aquatic vegetation, living or dead, that provides a degree of shelter for fish. Cover should not be confused with "structure," another catchword that refers to physical features such as drop-offs, points, large rocks, bridge pilings or docks. Water features include thermoclines, inflows and outflows, and seams and eddies, as well as other variations in current and depth.

While structure, food and water features may be situated anywhere within a body of water, rooted aquatic plants that make up the all-important "cover" are located only within the littoral zone. Since green plants cannot survive without sunlight for photosynthesis, the size and depth of the littoral zone is determined by the amount of sunlight that penetrates the water surface. Through photosynthesis, living green aquatic plants emit the oxygen essential for fish and other water-dwelling animals. Dead plants, however, remove oxygen from the water as they decompose. In eutrophic bodies of water, fly-rodders should avoid large areas of decaying vegetation because the dissolved oxygen levels may not be high enough for bass and other aquatic animals to survive.

The littoral zone supports a complex food web that is rich in plant and animal life. Herbivorous animals feed on the plants. Small carnivorous fish, insects and crustaceans, in turn, eat these herbivores, which in turn serve as food for larger predatory fish. Dead plants and animals that are not eaten will decompose and become nutrients for new plant growth as a body of water goes through its natural eutrophication process; thus, the food cycle continues. In typically healthy water like the St. Johns River, plants make up about 87 percent of all life. Aquatic animals (carnivores 3 percent and herbivores 10 percent) account for the remainder.

The littoral zone contains four communities of plant life: emergent plants, floating-leaf plants, submerged plants and wetland trees and shrubs. An understanding of them is essential to productive bass fishing on the St. Johns.

The St. Johns' Littoral Zone

The littoral zone of the St. Johns varies widely with seasonal water fluctuations, especially in the upper portion's vast lowlands, where I prefer to fish. During periods of low rainfall, the zone lies within the narrow confines of the riverbanks, but heavy precipitation can quickly raise the water level enough to extend the littoral area across the broad floodplain. When the St. Johns continues to rise during the rainy season, the littoral zone changes to the newly flooded sections of the river and ceases to exist in those once shallow areas where the water becomes too deep for sunlight to penetrate. This yearly rise and fall of water causes fish to migrate with the seasonal variations of rain and the resulting changes in the littoral zone. The largemouth population is concentrated when the river is low and the littoral zone is small, but as the water level rises and the littoral area expands, the fish become more scattered.

Emergent-Plant Subzone: Of the four subzones in the littoral zone, the emergent-plant subzone usually is found in the shallowest water — along the shoreline and around shallow bars. Here stems of plants extend well above the water, and the roots are anchored to the bottom. Cattails, pickerelweed, rushes, sedges and grasses are typical of emergent plants on the St. Johns. Florida's celebrated sunlight is most intense in these shallow waters, and the river's emergent plant sections usually provide the best fishing under low-light conditions, including mornings, evenings, nights and extremely cloudy days.

Because these plants are often located next to the riverbanks, the forage for bass there is diverse. The bass' diet includes not only aquatic animals, but also small land-based animals, including terrestrial insects (crickets and grasshoppers, for example), tiny mammals (mice), amphibians (frogs and salamanders) and reptiles (snakes and lizards). In this sub-

zone, a fly should be manipulated slowly so that it slides and climbs over and through the emergent vegetation. However, when the plant life is too thick to work the fly properly, casting to small pockets of open water within the subzone is more productive. Traditional bass-bugs and leech/eel imitations can be fished effectively with a floating line as long as they are tied to be truly weedless. Dragonfly and terrestrial imitations make excellent choices as well.

Floating-Leaf-Plant Subzone: This subzone generally lies just outside the emergent-plant subzone in slightly deeper water. Typical floating-leaf plants on the St. Johns include duckweeds, hyacinths, water lettuce and water lilies. Submerged plants may be scarce here because the floating-leaf plants frequently grow in large clusters and mats that significantly reduce the amount of light penetrating the water. But the surface cover also creates shade that attracts bass. During spawning season, this subzone is a favorite bedding area for largemouth bass and a variety of bream. Additionally, a number of insects and snails lay their eggs on the broad floating leaves, which provide the basis for an intricate food web that includes bass.

The V-shaped notch on the leaves of water lilies and spatterdock is a

A large portion of the St. Johns River still retains its picturesque "old-Florida" atmosphere.

Schools of sunshine and striped bass often feed alongside the largemouths, especially in the St. Johns' deep holes and around the mouths of its tributaries.

motion. And it's as exciting a strike as you'll find on the river.

Submerged-Plant Subzone: The submerged-plant subzone is located in the deepest part of the littoral zone on the outside edges of emergent and floating-leaf plants. Eelgrass and hornworts such as coontail, hydrilla and water millfoil are among the dominant plants.

The length and mass of submerged plants on the St. Johns and its lakes vary with the season. During the warm months, many of them, particularly the hornworts, grow so fast that they often form thick mats on the surface where there is little or no current. Under those conditions a floating line becomes essential, especially if the plants have many finely branched leaves like the prolific hydrilla, an exotic plant that has become a scourge throughout many of the state's bodies of water. A sinking line is just too difficult to fish in such heavy cover. To reduce the chances of entanglements, casts must be made to small openings in the lush vegetation.

I've always found a weedless popping bug to be the best type of fly in these situations, as even the most weedless sinking fly can foul when the water is completely choked with these plants. Nevertheless, any sort of line — sinking, intermediate, sink-tip or floater — can be used effectively when the plants are well below the surface or when the vegetation isn't too dense. In those situations, fish a weedless subsurface baitfish imitation either just above or through these plants.

Wetland Trees: A few trees can be found with their trunks rooted in the river's littoral zone. The submerged base and roots of these wetland trees, especially cypress, are excellent spots to look for largemouth bass. Flies should be presented as closely as possible to the tree base since the bass usually wait there for prey to either swim by or fall from limbs. A curve-cast can be used to effectively fish around the entire circumference of the trunk.

Other St. Johns Features

Although adequate cover is top priority when looking for largemouth bass on the St. Johns and its chain of lakes, many other daily variables must also be considered. One of the most important is what I call the shade factor. Bass like low-light conditions, which is why the best fishing usually occurs in the morning, evening, at night, on cloudy days, in cover and around structure. When the sun is shining, bass station themselves in the shade of objects and plants. That's where I concentrate most during daylight hours. Another prime area anglers often overlook is along deep-cut mud banks that are shaded from the sun. I have consistently taken some of my biggest largemouth from the edges of these dark, almost black, banks, particularly under overhanging vegetation.

One of my favorite times to fish the river system is after a rain. Bass will often gather near little rivulets, creek mouths, tributaries and other small openings where runoff flows into the main channel. Largemouth

notorious fly and fly-line grabber. To reduce the frustration of fishing in areas with these plants, I often opt for flies that have either round or conically shaped heads. These slide through the leaf notch, while a sharper-edged head might hang up. Floating lines and traditional bass-bugs are the mainstay in this subzone. However, a weighted leech/eel streamer can be combined with a sink-tip line and hopped along the bottom to mimic the Texas-rigged plastic worms anglers with bait-casting tackle use.

One of my favorite ways to fish for largemouth in this subzone is to strip a popper rapidly through a thick blanket of floating duckweed so abundant in many of the river's sloughs and attached lakes. Even though the popper may become fouled with duckweed, making it impossible for the bass to actually see the fly, the fish will strike ferociously at the com-

will also station themselves around cattle trails that drain rainfall into the river. Presentation should be made so that the fly appears to have been swept along by the tiny flow of water and into the main current.

Creek mouths and lake openings flowing into the river are prime places for schooling largemouth as well as stripers and sunshine bass. I usually anchor the boat or walk along the bank, waiting for the bass to show themselves on the surface as they attack groups of small finfish that also gather in the area. The mouths of Snake Creek, the Econolockhatchee, Deep Creek, the Wekiva and all lakes are open-water areas with only sparse vegetation to foul hooks. Poppers can produce some exciting topwater action, but Clouser Minnows are also deadly and will consistently take bass even when the fish aren't showing on the surface. When schoolies get selective — and they can at times — I rely on a sleek, quill-body popping bug tied by Bill Parlasca. He covers the quill with pearl mylar colored with pantone pens to look like a baitfish. Bass find it irresistible even when they refuse my other offerings, and I'm always grateful when Bill slides a couple of his specialties into my shirt pocket. Points, shoreline pockets and the edges of shallow bars are other spots to look for bass on the river.

Current is a factor, too. Bass usually avoid strong currents unless they are attacking schools of baitfish swimming along with the flow of water. Most of the time they prefer quiet water, including eddies and current edges or seams. Regardless of where the fish seem to be, fly-fishers should watch for a general behavior pattern and then look for it in other locations.

In the classic *Book of the Black Bass* (1881), Dr. James Henshall predicted that bass would become the "leading game fish of America," partly because they can prosper in a wide range of habitat. Henshall was right, of course. Today the largemouth bass is the No. 1 game species in the country, and its varied habitat includes lakes, ponds, small streams, estuaries and large rivers, all of which are contained within the St. Johns River system.

PLANNING A TRIP

The upper St. Johns River offers a wonderful blend of rare solitude, Florida history, uncommon beauty and outstanding fly-fishing for largemouth bass that leaves an unforgettable impression on first-time anglers as well as regular visitors. In addition to the great bass fishing, fly-fishers will find plenty of bluegills, sunfish, warmouth, specks (crappie), gar, mudfish (bowfin), pickerel, sunshine bass, shellcrackers and striped bass to keep their lines tight. And the winter run of American shad is just as outstanding. Anglers also occasionally encounter tarpon, redfish, ladyfish and other saltwater species that have ventured far upstream from the marine environment.

Anglers commonly see eagles, wild hogs, deer, black bears, otters, wild turkeys, manatees and roseate spoonbills along the river and its tributaries. The number and quality of bird rookeries are at least as good as or, in my opinion, better than any others in the state, including the more highly touted Everglades. History buffs will be interested in the ancient Indian mounds, Seminole battlegrounds, old paddlewheel riverboat landings and fossil beds that just a little investigation around the St. Johns will turn up. Other local outdoor adventures include riding an airboat on the river and fishing on the renowned flats of the nearby Indian River Lagoon system for redfish and seatrout. Bill Belleville's informative and beautifully written *River of Lakes: A Journey on Florida's St. Johns River* (2000) is a must-read for anyone who ventures onto this waterway.

Although fly-fishing guides can be hard to come by on the St. Johns, several marinas offer boat rentals for the do-it-yourselfer. Try the Lake Harney Marina in Geneva or Marina Isle in Sanford. For a unique experience, contact Travel Country Outdoors in Altamonte Springs to take a guided kayak trip down the Econlockahatchee and a portion of the St. Johns. A word of caution: Parts of the upper river can be a confusing maze to the unfamiliar. Take along a chart, a flashlight, extra water, insect repellent and a cell phone as precautions. Filing a float plan with a friend is a good idea, too.

The riverfront town of Sanford offers the best bet for a room, since several national chains operate there. Orlando and Titusville are reasonably close to the river, too. Campers can pitch their tents along some portions of the St. Johns. Mullet Lake Park in Sanford has camping sites and bathrooms, as does Blue Springs State Park near Orange City. Those looking for more civilized camping can stay at the KOA in Mims.

When hunger pangs strike, fill up on alligator tail, catfish and frog legs at rustic Black Hammock Restaurant in Oviedo, or try the fish sandwiches at the Osteen Bridge Restaurant in Sanford. Barbecue fans must visit Bubbalou's Bodacious Barbecue near the University of Central Florida in Oviedo for arguably the tastiest pork sandwiches, collard greens and sweet tea in the South. Rock shrimp and corn fritters are specialties of the house at Dixie Crossroads in Titusville.

For more information on the St. Johns River, see chapter 9 — "The St. Johns: Southernmost Shad."

CHAPTER 7

MOSQUITO COAST:
Tarpooms and Snukes

And here it comes; the tarpon breaks the surface, 100-plus pounds coming straight up out of the water like a shuttle launch, shaking and twisting, and when it lands again it is with the sound of a piano hitting the water.

— *Jim Fergus,* The Sporting Road, *1999*

I had just left the hangar, where the pilot had instructed me to reduce my luggage weight to only 25 pounds to help ensure that the plane would actually leave the ground on takeoff. Now, winding my way through a long gauntlet of junk fuselages and miscellaneous engine parts, my eyes were drawn toward a small and particularly worn-looking, single-engine airplane that is typical of those used in Third World countries. The plane looked like a salvaged conglomeration of the adjacent scraps, and I hoped it wasn't the one I would be flying in. It was.

As the pilot and I prepared to enter the plane, he caught me off guard. "We have a tradition of praying before every flight. Do you mind?"

It was a perfectly logical request, considering the condition of the plane, but even so, those were not words I wanted to hear from my pilot. I respectfully bowed my head, but my mind was on other things. Was the plane in such bad shape? Shouldn't he be checking the flaps or gas or something instead of calling on God to be our co-pilot? My destination had been described as a "heaven" for tarpon and snook. Had God somehow misunderstood?

Thankfully, the flight from Honduras' capital, Tegucigalpa, turned out to be uneventful, and as I clambered out of the tattered airplane onto the dirt runway near the village of Brus, I received a warm welcome from my hosts, the Thomas family, and a group of giggling Mosquito Indian children. Only when I over-heard the pilot's brief conversation with the Thomases did I realize he was a missionary who sometimes flew tourists to remote areas like this isolated out-

post on the Mosquito Coast. That helped explain the tradition of praying before takeoff and somewhat allayed my worries about the return trip. But I was still a little suspicious of that well-worn airplane.

I had come to Brus to fish the remote waters of Honduras' eastern coast, rumored to be loaded with big tarpon and snook. Until that time, not many fly-fishers had explored the region, and I relished the opportunity to cast flies in such a pristine fishery.

The Mosquito Coast hasn't changed much since Christopher Columbus landed there about 500 years ago. Mosquito Indians still live in primitive thatched huts, and there are no roads to connect the area with the outside world. Local travel is mostly by foot or "cayucu," a canoe fashioned from a single log. Jaguars, ocelots, tapirs and many rare and exotic birds reside nearby in the seemingly impenetrable Honduran jungle. Small streams originating in the virgin tropical rain forest of the Sierra de Esperanza Mountain Range flow through unspoiled coastal lowlands, where they merge with the sea to form delicate food-rich estuaries. These brackish bays, lagoons and coastal rivers are alive with shrimp, mullet, crabs and other small marine animals that form the forage base for large predatory fish. One of the largest estuaries on the Mosquito Coast is the greater Brus Lagoon system. Snook, some weighing more than 40 pounds, are plentiful in Brus Lagoon, but the dominant species in these waters is his majesty, the silver king.

Access to the fishing in Brus Lagoon was extremely limited until Dick Thomas and his family established a fishing lodge on Cannon Island, a small promontory of volcanic rock that stands out in stark contrast to the otherwise flat coastline. Although surrounded by salt water, the island has a freshwater well that makes it habitable. Like the Swiss Family Robinson, the Thomases have created a haven in this otherwise primitive wilderness. Accommodations are simple, yet comfortable. Guests sleep in one of the rustic cab-

Brus Lagoon

Honduras

TEGUCIGALPA

Big pods of giant tarpon gather regularly at the "bar mouth" of Brus Lagoon, where anglers armed with stout tackle can expect to jump numerous fish each day.

ins, and meals include a delicious mixture of Honduran and American dishes served in the main lodge. There is no air conditioning, but cabins do have private baths. Power comes from a gas-powered generator that goes off at 10 p.m. Most members of the lodge staff are local Mosquito Indians whose friendly demeanor makes guests feel comfortable and welcome.

I did, however, have one surprising encounter on the island. After leaving my cabin one morning to get breakfast, the Thomases' family pet, a cute white-faced monkey named Cocoa, fell from high up in a tree and landed inches from my feet with an audible "thud." The monkey appeared to be on the verge of death as it lay motionless and spread-eagled on the ground with eyes rolled back in its head. I ran frantically to the main lodge to get a family member, but, to my surprise, Dick smiled when told what had happened. "Damned monkey's been in the medi-

cine cabinet again," he chuckled. Apparently, the little devil was a drug addict, and the event was somewhat commonplace. Oh, the younger generation.

Dick Thomas' two sons, Bruce and Denny, handle most of the guiding duties in 20-foot, custom-made aluminum boats with seaworthy V-hulls, but the lodge employs native guides as well. Although there are extraordinary fly-fishing opportunities for snook and tarpon within a short boat ride of the lodge, Denny and Bruce are constantly exploring the vast lagoon and discovering new places to fish — an endless but pleasant task.

Brus Lagoon and Cannon Island have an interesting history. The island was a Spanish fortress until a battle with the Mosquito Indians in 1782, which the Spanish lost. A few Spanish cannons remain on the island as a reminder of the conflict, hence the name. "Brus" is a deriva-

Submerged structure and shallow sandbars outside the mouths of coastal rivers provide excellent hunting grounds for snook.

rivers, the first is a curious large fish, almost like a Salmon, the latter more like a Carp, with a big Bill or Mouth, and both very good to be eaten."

It's not uncommon to jump 12 or more tarpon a day in Brus Lagoon. Most weigh 60 to 125 pounds, although I hooked one that easily exceeded 150 pounds. Others whose word I respect claim to have seen larger. A few months after the lodge opened, an angler trolling with plugs caught a 210-pound specimen, and the guides talk of encounters with other 'poons of 200 pounds or more.

The best fishing can be found around the mouths of coastal waterways and inlets, but tarpon also inhabit quiet backcountry rivers. The guides' favorite spot is the Bar Mouth, a navigable, albeit somewhat treacherous, opening that connects the lagoon with the open sea. The heaviest concentrations of tarpon, and many of the biggest fish, typically hold in the vicinity of this pass. I jumped many fish there every day, with the best fishing usually on the sea outside the pass. However, strong winds and rough water sometimes made it impossible to stand and cast from a boat, so on those occasions we fished in the relative calm inside the Bar Mouth or in one of the coastal rivers.

In contrast to the vast open reaches of water around the Bar Mouth, the coastal rivers and waterways provide a vista of lush jungle, exotic fauna and slow-moving dark water. Here, the placid surface is interrupted only by the reflective flashes of rolling tarpon or the explosive launch of one that is hooked. According to Denny Thomas, rainfall and water flow greatly influence tarpon movement, and historically some rivers seem to hold more tarpon than others.

Although most of the fly-fishing here requires blind-casting into dark water from 8 to 25 feet deep, you'll also find ample opportunities for sight fishing for tarpon swimming near the surface of the open sea or in the clear shallows adjoining ocean inlets.

Snook inhabit many of the same areas of Brus Lagoon as tarpon, but while the tarpon generally prefer open water, snook hang close to structure along shoreline vegetation, near deep-cut banks or among the tangled limbs of submerged deadfalls. But many also reside in open water around surf lines, inlets and coastal rivers.

Because Brus Lagoon is a relatively new destination for fly-fishers, the guides are still learning the peculiar ways of their clients. Although the lodge maintains a small inventory of fly-tying supplies and a marginal amount of tackle, an angler planning to visit the area should bring along everything he'll need.

A rod with a powerful butt section gives anglers a real advantage for the kind of deepwater tarpon fishing they will encounter around Brus Lagoon. That's because the fish usually stay on the bottom after the first few jumps, and then the battle becomes a lifting contest for the angler. I recommend having at least two outfits on hand for these tarpon — a 10- or 11-weight and a 12- or 13-weight. The lighter outfit gets most of my

tive of Brewster, the surname of the pirate Bloody Brewster, who once sailed these waters. Although the area is just beginning to gain notoriety with fly-fishers as a hot spot for tarpon and snook, early travelers also marveled at the sheer numbers of these two great game fish in Brus Lagoon. One such visitor, whose name has been lost to history, wrote in his diary in 1699: "Tarpooms and Snukes are thick on the seawaves and

attention while blind-casting, but once we've located big fish I'll switch to stronger tackle. While the 10- or 11-weight rod usually lacks the fish-fighting capabilities of a heavier stick, it will handle average-sized tarpon and is a lot easier to cast for an extended length of time. Nevertheless, I wouldn't want to be holding anything less than a 12-weight during a confrontation with a 200-pound tarpon.

A Type IV sinking shooting head is ideal for most of the tarpon fishing, especially in deep water. I prefer to attach it to a 30- to 35-pound-test monofilament running line, although a traditional fly line running line of 35-pound-test is also a good choice. When fish are near the surface or in shallow water, a slow-sinking monocore works well. Reels should hold 250 yards or more of backing. An 80- to 100-pound shock tippet must be attached to the class tippet section of standard big-game leaders.

Since visibility is limited in many areas of the lagoon, tarpon detect fully dressed flies like Whistlers more easily because these displace, or "push," more water than sparsely dressed patterns. Any good selection of flies should include combinations of red-and-white, red-and-yellow and black-and-red in sizes 3/0 to 5/0. Plan to go through a lot of flies during a week's stay at Cannon Island. Extra fly lines are a good idea, too.

For snook, a 9- or 10-weight rod matched to a reel holding around 200 yards of backing will prove necessary. That may seem a little heavier than is ordinarily used for these fish, but the large overall size of the local snook and the heavy concentration of submerged structure require stouter tackle. Leaders should have a 40- to 50-pound monofilament shock tippet to prevent the snook's sharp gill covers from cutting the line. When blind-casting for snook in water where tarpon also congregate, I used 10-weight tackle with an 80-pound shock tippet just in case I hooked a tarpon instead of a snook — a rather common occurrence.

The same Whistler patterns used for tarpon also work for snook, and any good selection of flies should also include Lefty's Deceivers and Clouser Deep Minnows, as well as a few deer-hair poppers and sliders in various sizes and colors. Even though a Type IV shooting head is ideal for prospecting for snook in open water, it may result in frequent hang-

ups and lost flies if used around the log jams and submerged structures that fill many of these waters. In those situations, a floating line is more practical. No matter which line you use, a weed guard should be considered essential for any fly fished near cover.

According to Denny and Bruce Thomas, the Mosquito Coast offers a year-round fishery for both tarpon and snook, but November and December usually see the peak of the rainy season. Weight and space limitations make it imperative to pack wisely for a trip to Cannon Island. Lightweight pants, shorts and shirts are essential in the torrid Honduran heat. The lodge provides daily laundry service, so guests need only a minimum amount of clothing. I got by with two shirts, one pair of pants and two pairs of shorts with mesh liners, along with other necessities, such as a raincoat, hat and sunscreen. That left room under my 25-pound weight limit for essential heavy items like fly reels and cameras and for my space-saving multipiece fly rods.

Prayer books are optional.

Cannon Island Lodge was built on a volcanic island on Honduras' Mosquito Coast, one of the most remote regions in Central America.

PLANNING A TRIP

The only way to get to Cannon Island is to book through a reputable adventure travel agent authorized by the Thomases. The logistics and complications of getting to Honduras and then to the Mosquito Coast are complicated and best left in the hands of a professional. You'll find little to do on the Mosquito Coast other than enjoy the wonderful unspoiled surroundings, exotic wildlife, primitive native Indians and, of course, the fishing. But that's the purpose of going, isn't it? The truly adventurous can visit Mayan ruins, discovered and even undiscovered in the thick jungle. Cigar aficionados should grab a few highly rated Honduran brands at the airport to smoke during their stay.

A trip to Cannon Island can be combined with an excursion to the island of Guanaja, where good numbers of permit roam the flats and adjacent waters offer world-class skin and scuba diving.

CHAPTER 8

SENEGAL
Big Game on the Dark Continent

Hurricanes start when a slight kink — a disturbance in the trade winds, a dust storm blowing out to sea off the Sahara — develops in the upper-level air.

— *Sebastian Junger,* The Perfect Storm, *1997*

The sea air was thick with sandy dust that had blown in from the Sahara — perhaps the beginning of some yet-to-be-named tropical storm that would greet me days later when I returned home to Florida. A fresh, thin layer of the fine dirt covered the surface of everything exposed to the atmosphere, and the sun appeared only as a dim globe aloft in the eerie golden mist. From the back of our chartered boat, Dave Perkins and I stared across the rolling blue surface of the Atlantic Ocean near Cap Vert, Africa. We had come for an African big-game experience. Neither of us would be disappointed.

Big-game animals such as Serengetti lions, Congo Basin elephants, Nile crocodiles and mountain gorillas have become nearly synonymous with Africa. While these predators dominate the savannas and jungles, less celebrated and more obscure types of big game roam the blue waters along the continent's western tip at the Cap Vert Peninsula. There, concentrations of large pelagic fishes seasonally gather within the fertile depths of the eastern Atlantic Ocean, most notably marlin and sailfish. The lion may be king of the jungle, but these two billfish rule Africa's marine environment. They also offer outstanding opportunities to the fly-fisher who pursues giant oceanic fish with a long and slender rod.

Within the realm of fly-fishing, the waters of the open sea are the newest frontier. Dr. Webster Robinson, Lee Cuddy, Lee Wulff, Lefty Reagan and Harry Kime were at the forefront of offshore fly-fishing, but the sport is still in its developmental stages, and its ranks of anglers are growing rapidly. Consequently, fly-fishing methods and tackle are constantly being refined, and new destinations seem to be discovered regularly. Current popu-lar spots include Costa Rica, Baja and Guatemala, but the lesser-known waters of West Africa also rank among the best in the world.

Coastal West Africa includes the westernmost bulge of the continent, where the warm currents from the Gulf of Guinea Stream act as a migratory highway for game fish and their prey. Nowhere on the coast does this current come closer to shore than at the Cap Vert Peninsula, a long arm of land that juts far out into the sea at the port city of Dakar, Senegal. Cap Vert's unique geographic location and peninsular shape have placed it in the center of some of the world's best billfishing.

The peninsula is virtually surrounded on its three sides by excellent offshore fly-fishing opportunities. Sails, marlin and other offshore fishes concentrate in specific areas, which local anglers call "zones," on each side of the peninsula. Zone 1 lies to the north of Cap Vert, while zones 2 and 3 lie to the west and south respectively. Zones 1 and 2 are good bets for both sails and marlin. Zone 3 is almost exclusively a sailfish fishery that offers outstanding opportunities year round. We concentrated on zones 1 and 2 since those areas seemed the most productive during our stay.

Sailfish — often referred to as *espadon voilier* by Senegal's French-speaking populace and *naw naw* in the native Wolof tongue — are the most sought-after game fish along the Cap Vert Peninsula. Concentrations of sails are heaviest from June to September, but excellent fishing often continues well into November.

Most of the sailfish we caught weighed approximately 50 pounds, and a few topped 70; however, even larger fish move into these waters around the beginning of September when some specimens exceed 90 pounds. Although the Atlantic strain of sailfish is generally smaller than its Pacific cousin, the average fish along Africa's west coast has proven much larger than those I've encountered anywhere else in the Atlantic. Fly-fishers looking to set world records for Atlantic sailfish will be hard-pressed to find a place with more potential than the water surrounding Cap Vert.

DAKAR

Senegal

© NEAL & LINDA ROGERS

Africa's big-game animals aren't restricted to its jungles and savannas. Large pelagic game fish, including marlin and sailfish, abound in its offshore currents.

© TIMOTHY O'KEEFE

Anglers fishing these waters will be just as impressed with the number of fish as with the average size. On each trip to the Gulf of Guinea Stream, we regularly attracted sails. On the best days we easily raised more than a dozen fish, and generally they were aggressive and came readily to the fly. Gary Sherman, an experienced angler who accompanied us on this trip, says that he has consistently raised more than 20 sails per trip since he first began exploring these waters in 1978.

Regardless of those substantial numbers, anglers must remember that fly-fishing for sails rarely involves constant fishing action. Rather, intervals of waiting, watching and searching are only infrequently interrupted by periods of pandemonium. Dave and I sometimes used the lulls in action to replenish our leader supply and to re-rig tackle damaged in a previous struggle.

During our last few days in Africa, vast schools of sardines moved into the area, and packs of sailfish rounded up the small fish into tight clusters, an instinctive routine commonly referred to as "balling the bait." However, in the midst of all the natural bait, the sails became surprisingly selective, and even though the fish would occasionally move in behind the spread of artificial teasers, they

Fast sailfish action is the norm in the Gulf of Guinea Stream around Cap Vert, on Africa's westernmost thumb near the city of Dakar.

There are two peak seasons for blues — May through July, when the fish migrate from south to north, and September through November, when cooler temperatures send the marlin back south. The blues commonly weigh in the 300-pound range, though anglers generally catch the biggest fish, up to 800 pounds, during the fall run.

We hoped to tease some small, fly-rod-sized blues to the boat, but only two extremely large fish — one that easily topped 500 pounds and another that was only slightly smaller — showed a half-hearted interest in the trolled baits. It was just as well, since neither of us relished a long and probably unsuccessful fight with one of those behemoths.

Although the offshore fly-fishing can be fantastic around the Cap Vert Peninsula, charter services remain limited, especially those that can accommodate fly-fishers. For the most part, the charter crews are still learning some of the idiosyncrasies of offshore fly-fishing, although they can skillfully rig baits and tease fish to the boat. Nevertheless, what the crews lack in experience they more than make up for in enthusiasm. Besides, there are plenty of fish to practice on — and in the game of fly-fishing for sailfish, the tease itself is as much fun as the catch.

generally wouldn't stay interested for long. Borrowing from the trout fisherman's match-the-hatch philosophy, we caught some of the sardines and rigged them to use as natural baits for trolling and teasing. The result: The sailfish teased into a frenzy and struck our flies without hesitation.

Because of the great numbers of sailfish, fly-fishers often neglect the opportunity to pursue the more difficult and infrequent blue marlin.

This type of fishing requires a coordinated team effort between angler and crew. We typically trolled three "natural" hookless teaser baits, along with a spreader rig of artificial lures. When we raised a billfish, the crew removed all baits from the water, except for the primary teaser bait. Just before the cast, the skipper moved the gear to neutral and allowed suffi-

IF YOU NEED IT, BRING IT

You won't find any fly shops in the city of Dakar, so bring you own equipment. A 12-weight rod combined with a reel that holds at least 250 yards of 30-pound backing will suffice for sailfish as well as other incidental species, including yellowfin tuna and wahoo. Tackle for marlin should include a 15-weight or heavier fly rod paired with a reel that holds 500 or more yards of backing. I also suggest a 10-weight outfit for dolphin and other medium-sized game fish that frequent Senegal's offshore waters.

Big-game (or tarpon)-style leaders, with a class tippet section attached to a 100-pound-test monofilament shock leader, are standard for sailfish, marlin and most other oceanic fishes. Double-hooked "Big Bird" or "flying chicken"-style flies with foam popping heads work well for billfish. Because of the sheer numbers of fish available in these waters, you'll need plenty of flies. Choose hook sizes between 4/0 and 6/0, depending on whether you're after sailfish or marlin. I generally prefer Owner hooks, or close facsimiles, because their unique point readily penetrates a billfish's tough mouth. And bring some single-hooked patterns, such as Lefty's Deceivers and Clouser Minnows, for dorado and other pelagics.

SIGHTS TO SEE

In addition to its great fly-fishing for billfish, Senegal has an interesting history, a rich culture and an abundance of natural resources. Formerly a part of French West Africa, Senegal gained its independence in 1960. The coastal city of Dakar has a long fishing history, as evidenced by the brightly painted traditional fishing boats that local artisans have hand-crafted for generations. The strangely beautiful Goree Island, whose prisons were once at the center of the African slave trade, is easily viewed from the high bluffs of Dakar. On each trip to and from the fishing grounds, one cannot pass by Goree without reflecting on the island's gruesome past and on man's inhumanity to man. In contrast, today's Dakar is a modern city whose friendly people and wonderful bustling markets belie its terrible past.

Naturally, visitors will want to set aside time to tour this unique country, where shopping and sight-seeing opportunities are seemingly endless. Gourmands can enjoy wonderfully prepared French cuisine at one of the many restaurants owned by French ex-patriots. For the more adventuresome, there's Niokolo-Koba National Park in the eastern part of the country where lions, elephants and other African wildlife can be seen. Visitors will want to take plenty of photos, but keep in mind that a large percentage of the Senegalese are Muslims who, because of religious beliefs, become upset if their picture is taken.

A side trip to Senegal's Niokolo-Koba National Park will give visitors a chance to view exotic African animals in their natural setting.

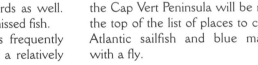

cient time for the boat to coast to a stop so that the fly wouldn't be "trolled" when it hit the water. Language differences initially made it difficult for Dave and me to communicate with the crew, but even so, we worked well together following "practice runs" on the first few fish. After several days, I even managed to develop a very limited Wolof vocabulary, and the African crew had learned some English words as well. Unfortunately, most were the expletives that we hurled at missed fish.

Before the beginning of the 20th century, Africa was frequently referred to as the "Dark Continent" because it remained a relatively unexplored and mysterious frontier. While the interior of Africa has long since been opened to tourism, its offshore waters remain largely untapped by fly-fishers. As the number of offshore fly-fishing devotees continues to grow rapidly, the cobalt-colored ocean currents along the Cap Vert Peninsula will be near the top of the list of places to catch Atlantic sailfish and blue marlin with a fly.

PLANNING A TRIP

The logistics of arranging an offshore fly-fishing trip to Africa can be difficult and frustrating. Fortunately, some potential problems can be eliminated by booking a trip through Air Afrique, a first-rate airline that makes daily nonstop flights between New York and Dakar. The airline also owns the Air Afrique Sportfishing Center with its fleet of five professionally maintained 28-foot Bertrams, and can further accommodate customers by reserving a room at Dakar's beautiful Hotel Teranga. The result is hassle-free traveling for the fly-fisher who wants to test Senegal's outstanding billfishing.

Fly-fishers can also charter a 31-foot Bertram operated by Cyril Calendini in Dakar. Calendini's family owns Le Lagon, an outstanding waterfront hotel and restaurant.

Ground transportation is readily available in one of Dakar's many inexpensive taxis. However, to avoid any dispute later, be sure to negotiate the fare before the ride.

You'll need a passport to enter Senegal, and wise travelers will consult their local health department for information on suggested immunization. A final word of caution: Drink only bottled water to prevent potential problems.

CHAPTER 9

ST. JOHNS RIVER:
Southernmost Shad

In the South, when wading and casting flies for shad, I had heard innumerable derogatory comments, but I was surprised to hear from a big outboard cruiser the following: "Look at that damned tourist with the fly pole. Watch me gun this hooker and fill his rubber pants full of water!"

— *Charley Waterman*, Field Days, 1995

As the sky took on the golden glow of a late winter afternoon, wakes, boils and surface thrashing continuously agitated the normally placid surface of Florida's St. Johns River. American shad and an occasional hickory shad were in the midst of an orgasmic water dance that they deliriously perform every day at this time of year as part of an annual spawning ritual. The water was alive with their excitement.

My companion, Bill Parlasca, and I had just put away our rods to silently watch the frenzy. The previous three hours had been happily spent with bent rods, tight lines and lots of shad leaping from the water with our flies dangling from their lips. Now, as reverent spectators, we paused to witness the creation of another generation of fish that we hoped would eventually give us as much pleasure as those we had caught and released on this exceptional day.

Each year, one of the most prolific yet little known runs of anadromous fish occurs during the winter months in east-central Florida as shad make their annual migration from the sea to spawn near the headwaters of the St. Johns River. Approximately 90 percent of the fish are American shad; the remainder are the closely related but smaller hickory shad.

Shad spend four to five years in salt water before returning to spawn in the rivers where they were born. Florida has the southernmost migration, and recovered tags indicate that shad returning to the St. Johns travel from as far away as Canada's Bay of Fundy.

The American, or white, shad is the largest of the herrings. In Florida, they average 2 to 3 pounds, and 5-pounders are caught with regularity. Hickories average 1 to 1 1/2 pounds. In the rivers of more northern states along the Eastern Seaboard, the average size of American shad is slightly larger than in Florida, probably because some of the northern fish are repeat spawners. Those in the St. Johns die after reproducing — mostly the result of making such an exhaustively long trip, but probably also because the warm southern river drains the fish of the energy necessary for a return to the Atlantic.

The run on the St. Johns usually begins in early December when the water begins to cool considerably. Male shad, or bucks, are the first to arrive, followed shortly by the larger females, or roe shad. The height of activity occurs in January, February and March when water temperatures hover in the mid-60s, but shad often remain well into April.

Like other anadromous fish that have to make long oceanic migrations to spawn in fresh water, American shad are strong and determined fighters that do not come easily to the net. Also adding to the difficulty is their thin membranous mouth that is fragile and easily torn by fly-fishers who apply too much pressure during an encounter. Once hooked, shad become flashing silvery missiles that launch themselves repeatedly from the water between bursts of acceleration. These characteristics have earned them the nickname "poor man's salmon," but I feel they look and act almost like baby tarpon.

Though the American shad remains a comparatively unknown North American game fish, its roots are deeply planted in angling history. Sportsmen have chased them for well over 150 years, and their regional popularity on the eastern seaboard led noted fly-fisher and fisheries culturist Seth Green to transplant the species to several rivers on the West Coast. They now flourish from northern California to British Columbia.

The migratory run begins at the mouth of the St. Johns near Jacksonville. Once the fish enter the

Jacksonville

St. Johns River

Florida

Sanford

Orlando

Deep-cut banks with a strong current create primary gathering spots for shad, which resemble baby tarpon in appearance as well as in fighting characteristics.

river, they make their way toward the upper reaches where the environment is ideal for spawning. The most productive section lies between Lake Monroe, near the town of Sanford, and Highway 50 to the south. Shad gather there because 80 percent of the river's fall occurs within this 60-mile stretch, and the resulting strong currents keep the fish's eggs from settling in the bottom silt where they may perish. But shad can also be found in other locales along the river, as well as in large tributaries. The best places to fish are in the main channel around deep banks and holes scoured out by the current. In times of low water, the shad increasingly tend to gravitate toward the river's upper reaches. Some popular gathering places for shad include the areas around Lemon Bluff, Marina Isle, Highway 50 and Puzzle Lake.

Anglers need a small boat to reach the best shad spots since access is limted for those fishing from the bank. Peak fishing time runs between

During the peak of the shad run, it is not uncommon to catch-and-release 50 or more good-sized fish per day. Preferred flies during this time include flashy, weighted flies tied to ride in an inverted position.

late morning and late afternoon.

Anything from a 3- to a 7-weight outfit will work on St. Johns shad. An 8 1/2- to 9-foot rod matched to a light, inexpensive reel makes a good combination. Depending on water conditions, any sort of line from a floater to high-density sinking heads will effectively catch fish. In average water depths, I prefer sink-tip lines. When water levels are high and accompanied by relatively strong currents, opt for sinking shooting heads. Floating lines can prove indispensable during periodic droughts. A tapered leader approximately 7 1/2 feet long works for all lines,

SPECIALTY SHAD FLIES

While at sea, the shad's diet consists almost entirely of phytoplankton and zooplankton, including minute crustaceans, fish eggs, insects and algae. The fish swims with its mouth open and gills flared as it strains food from the water. Spawners don't feed while in fresh water but they readily strike properly presented and specially adapted flies. Flashy flies weighing approximately 1/32 ounce are the most productive. Red-and-white, blue-and-white, silver-and-red, yellow, chartreuse and orange are all good colors, especially when tied with brilliant, reflective materials like Krystal Flash, Mylar or Flashabou.

The best patterns are weighted with either bead-chain or dumbbell eyes positioned on the top of the hook shank so that the fly rides in an inverted position. Near the bottom where the shad are located, inverted patterns can be worked with fewer hang-ups than standard patterns. Use bullet heads if necessary to add weight to a fly.

The shad's small mouth will require Mustad hooks 3906 and 9672 or equivalents in sizes 6 and 8. Favorite local patterns include Red-Headed Killer, Tom's Shad Fly, St. John's Shad Fly and Timbuctoo. Sometimes the fish will key in on a particular pattern, while other times almost any bright streamer will draw strikes. I use a Red-Headed Killer almost exclusively year in and year out, but a friend of mine did surprisingly well with a Crazy Charlie bonefish fly after he ran out of shad patterns.

Because their migratory seasons coincide, great flocks of white pelicans congregate along the St. Johns when the run is on, adding to the spectacular setting.

although some fly-fishers prefer a shorter length with a sinking line.

Make casts either at a 90-degree angle to the current or just slightly downstream and across. To allow the fly sufficient time to sink, dead-drift it with an occasional upstream mend until it's quartering downstream. Then strip the fly slow enough to occasionally feel it bumping on the bottom. Anything faster usually significantly reduces the number of strikes.

When shad strike reluctantly or when they continuously follow a fly without taking, I sometimes employ a method I call "doodle socking." If no strike occurs after retrieving the fly about halfway through a spot that holds fish, I feed about 5 feet of slack line back into the current so that the fly drifts freely. Then I slowly begin stripping the fly again. Sometimes I'll repeat this procedure several times to entice a strike. On many days, it has proven to be the most effective way to catch fish.

During the height of an average year's shad run, it's not at all uncommon to catch 15 or more fish in a day. During exceptional migrations, 50 fish a day is a real possibility. Few waters can provide that kind of fly-fishing excitement. Fortunately, almost all of the fly-rodders I encounter on the St. Johns have long been converted to catch-and-release fishing. Since a single female can produce around 30,000 eggs, the fishery's future should be assured for generations to come.

PLANNING A TRIP

Finding good shad fishing spots on the St. Johns River isn't difficult during an average run, but a boat is needed to access most of the best fishing. Boat rentals are available from Marina Isle Fish Camp and Lake Harney Fish Camp on State Road 46 east of the town of Sanford.

Plenty of accommodations are offered in nearby Sanford. Its location on the banks of the St. Johns River makes it the ideal headquarters for serious shad anglers. Those looking for bright lights and glitter will find plenty about a half-hour's drive south in Orlando.

For more information on the St. Johns River, see Chapter 6 — "Welaka: River of Lakes."

CHAPTER 10

NORTH ISLAND:

Travels with the Ghost of Zane Grey

Beautiful New Zealand! I gazed over those bold clear-cut ranges toward the north, where I had left the Kara Kara Islands and the Cavallis, and far to the interior, the green-white Tongariro River. How strange to love places so quickly! But love is not a matter of time. Again I wondered if I would ever come back. How many lovely places in the world to find and know! How many millions of lovely places one can never see!

— Zane Grey, Tales of the Angler's Eldorado, New Zealand, 1926

The interior rivers and surrounding coastline of New Zealand's beautiful North and South Islands provide an incredible array of exceptional fly-fishing opportunities, all relatively close to one another. There are so many outstanding places to cast flies in both salt and fresh water that fly-fishers are eventually faced with the pleasant, although sometimes perplexing, task of choosing where to start. At least you can be confident that if fishing action is slow in one location, another prime fishery is only a short distance away.

Earliest publications extolling New Zealand's outstanding fly-fishing include W.H. Spackman's *Trout in New Zealand, Where to Go and How to Catch Them* (1892) and the more in-depth *Trout Fishing and Sport in Maoriland* by G.D. Hamilton (1904). Although the material is somewhat dated, both books make interesting reading, especially the Hamilton chapters that eloquently describe hundreds of the country's lakes and streams. But it wasn't until Zane Grey recounted his visit to the North Island in *Tales of the Angler's Eldorado, New Zealand* (1926) that equal coverage was given to both trout and saltwater fisheries.

Grey's base of operations for his marine fishing excursions was near the northernmost tip of the North Island at Whangaroa Harbour near the Cavalli Islands. His trout fishing trips included legendary waters of the Tongariro River and Lake Taupo. It was these

adventures that were on my mind as my 20-some-hour-long plane ride from hell finally ended at the Auckland airport. I hoped to roughly follow in Grey's footsteps as I sampled the best of what the Kiwis have to offer.

Cavalli Islands

The 65-foot charter boat stopped just outside the breaking surf, and now it was my turn to get off. The mate lowered a small inflatable dinghy over the side, threw in several large boxes of frozen burly, or chum, and climbed inside. I followed him with an armful of fly gear and took a seat near the front of the tiny boat along with two other fly-fishermen. The next few minutes were reminiscent of a Class III whitewater scene from *Deliverance*, without the dueling banjos and squealing pig. Things got a little dicey as the mate deftly maneuvered the dinghy through breaking waves, protruding rocks and treacherous currents before dropping us on one of the many desolate rocky isles that make up the Cavalli Islands.

Once we got settled onshore, the mate immediately set up a huge, continuous chum slick with the burly, and the fish didn't take long to find it. An enormous school of kahawai (sounds like "ka-ha-why") roiled the surface, drawn by the oily fish bits swept along in the strong tidal current. It reminded me of an excerpt from *Angler's Eldorado* in which Grey describes seeing "acres of kahawai." I scrambled to a rocky promontory at the edge of the water just above the heaving sea and made a long cast with a sinking shooting head that landed in front of the rapidly advancing dark mass of fish. The line tightened on the first quick strip.

The take was so hard and fast that the running line slightly burned the crease in the first joint of my right index finger before I could let go. The kahawai's powerful initial run culminated in an arching salmonlike jump followed by another strong surge and leap before the fish headed toward the bottom for a

Cavalli Islands
•Whangaroa
Harbour

AUCKLAND

North Island

Lake
Taupa

New Zealand

South Island

more dogged battle. Fighting the fish from the high stationary position was exhilarating, with waves breaking violently on the rocks below me. I could taste the salty spray on my lips as I gingerly played the kahawai on 6-pound tippet.

A new dilemma suddenly developed when the fish began to tire. How was I going to land it in the high, crashing surf without putting myself in a precarious situation? Looking around, I spotted a quiet tidal pool several yards away, where the water was much calmer, and decided to carefully work my way across the slick, jagged rocks and rough surf to catch and subsequently release the fish there. The plan worked, and as I paused to free the fish, I could see that my newfound companions were engaged in the pandemonium as well. Surprisingly, the action didn't bother the rest of the school as we continued to cast into its midst.

During the course of the day, one big school of kahawai would swim into the burly only to eventually lose interest and be replaced by another. I have never seen such great rafts of fish in my life. By the time the mothership returned late in the afternoon, I had revisited the small tidal pool scores of times during consistent action throughout the day. If Zane Grey's ghost maintains a presence in these waters, I'm sure it's because the fishing may be just as good as when he cruised the Cavallis.

The Cavalli Islands are an isolated volcanic archipelago of rugged stone monoliths situated on the northeast tip of North Island. Their naked black shores stand in stark contrast to the fertile blue waters that meander and crash wildly amongst the rocky projections. The offshore currents of the Pacific are also nearby and pass closer to the mainland here than in any other part of the country. This unique marine environment attracts a wide variety of game fish, everything from tiny jack mackerel to blue marlin. But it's the kahawai that provide consistent fly-fishing excitement throughout the year.

There are two closely related species of kahawai, but *Arripis trutta* is the one commonly found in New Zealand waters. Both are sometimes referred to as "Australian salmon," probably because of their similar shape and steel-gray color, although they are not related to any of the salmonids. These fish may exceed 30 pounds in rare instances, but mostly fall in the 4- to 8-pound range, with the occasional kahawai topping 10 pounds.

The beautifully rugged Cavalli Islands near Zane Grey's former encampment at Whangaroa Harbour attract huge schools of kahawai during the flood tide.

The native Maori people are responsible for the fish's name, which in English means "white water." The name probably either refers to the splashing surface commotion made by schooling fish or pertains to the foam-edged shorelines where the fish congregate. Kahawai are pelagic fishes that favor inshore over offshore waters. They especially like rocky areas, like those in the Cavallis.

Kahawai have a varied diet that includes mostly small fishes such as pilchards and anchovies, but at times they will also consume tiny marine crustaceans, or "krill." Diving birds and surface feeding frenzies are indications of schooling kahawai. A Clouser Minnow thrown into the melee will almost always draw a strike, although the fish aren't particularly selective and will take any number of small to medium-sized flies, including topwater poppers pulled quickly through the water. Fly patterns

GEARING UP FOR KAHAWAI

Tackle requirements for kahawai are simple. I like an 8- or 9-weight rod with a reel that holds about 150 to 200 yards of backing plus 100 feet of running line and a shooting head. Unless you're throwing a topwater fly, a high-density shooting line is the best choice. As with all shooting-head setups, use a 30-foot-long head about one or two line weights heavier than the rod designation to properly flex the rod. For this kind of fishing, I strongly prefer a braided monofilament running line instead of those made of single-strand mono or small-diameter fly line. The braided line tangles less and isn't as easily nicked on the rocks as the single-strand type. It also casts farther than the fly-line version.

Since kahawai don't spook easily, long leaders aren't necessary. A 7 1/2-foot tapered leader is a good match for floating lines, while substantially shorter ones can be used with sinking shooting heads. Tippets between 6- and 12-pound test prove the most practical, but some fly-fishers prefer to use heavier tippets in case bigger species, like the highly-prized "kingfish" (a local nickname for the southern yellowtail), move into the area — a rather common occurrence. Although kahawai don't have sharp teeth, a 30-pound-test shock tippet will protect the lighter mono from the constant wear and tear of catching a high number of fish.

Even though the northeast part of North Island is considered subtropical, the weather can change rapidly and the sea air can get cool at times, especially in the mornings and evenings. I bought one of the fine shirts made of New Zealand's world-famous wool to use as an outer layer on such occasions, but a polar fleece jacket works just as well. Rogue waves and water spray from the crashing surf will often get clothes damp and sometimes will even downright drench them. Quick-drying pants and shirts are beneficial in those situations. I also recommend bringing an extra pair of nonslip deck shoes along in case one pair wears out after several days of fishing on the sharp, wet rocks. Rain gear should be a part of any excursion, too.

should be highly durable and able to withstand several battles so that they won't need to be replaced when the action is most hectic.

Kahawai are extremely popular with saltwater fly-fishers Down Under. That's partly because their population is so great and they are relatively easy to access, but it's also the result of the fishes' willingness to take flies as well as their impressive fighting qualities when hooked. They possess all of the hallmark characteristics of great game fish: strength, stamina, speed and aerial acrobatics.

Probably the best place to access the Cavallis is out of the picturesque little town of Whangaroa Harbour, a throwback to the early part of the 20th century when Zane Grey fished here. The historic settlement has several charter services, and accommodations are available at a handful of quaint lodges, including the exquisite Kingfish Lodge built at the site of Grey's original fishing camp. Only a few of the charter crews have any fly-fishing expertise, so it pays to call ahead and ask questions before booking a trip. Guests of the Kingfish Lodge can have the staff make all fly-fishing arrangements.

The most inexpensive and, I believe, most exciting way to fly-fish in the Cavallis is by hiring a boat that taxis anglers back and forth from the rocky islands. The crews know which isles normally have the best fishing, but it pays to discuss special fly-fishing needs ahead of time to avoid problems and disappointments later. At a minimum, make sure you fish a beach where the wind isn't in your face and where there's plenty of room for a backcast. Another vital feature for any drop-off spot is an elevation that offers protection above the high tide mark and breaking waves. Less adventurous fly-fishers can enlist a charter boat for an entire day of casting from the relative safety of a large vessel with amenities like comfortable seats and a head. During inclement weather, Whangaroa's sheltered harbor can provide good action, although the fishing is not of the same caliber as that in the Cavalli Islands.

For most fly-fishers, New Zealand conjures up visions of temperamental trout in cold, misty rivers, and rightfully so. The Kiwis have one of the premier rainbow and brown trout fisheries in the world. Still, people who are so totally focused on freshwater salmonids that they overlook the shoreline opportunities are missing some of the best fly-fishing New Zealand has to offer.

The Interior

Peter Scott and I hit it off right away. We met while fly-fishing in the Cavallis, where our mutual passion for fly-fishing led to several evenings of long discussions over local oysters and Steinlagers at the Kingfish Bar. At the time, Peter was trying to establish a full-time guide service for trout fishermen. As a former guide myself, I offered some suggestions. I was simultaneously picking his brain, while he shared his knowledge about some largely untapped rivers where I might fly-fish for rainbows and

browns during the rest of my stay in New Zealand. At the end of our saltwater fly-fishing trip in the Cavallis, Peter generously offered to chauffeur me around his native country. At his suggestion, we were going to forego the popular and relatively crowded Tongariro River and Lake Taupo touted by Zane Grey and instead investigate the country's other outstanding waters.

After an early start the next day, Peter gave me a running history of New Zealand as we toured native Maori settlements, volcanic mountains, subtropical "bush" and the almost endless green rolling pastures with their white patches of grazing sheep. I enjoyed the commentary, but I also was amazed at the number of rivers we passed, most of which receive little or no fishing pressure, according to Peter. At midmorning we turned onto a winding gravel road that paralleled one such obscure stream — the Waipa.

The Waipa isn't some newly discovered fly-fishing mecca. As a matter of fact, I'm sure other rivers in North Island offer better fly-fishing. Furthermore, there is really nothing that would especially distinguish it

The number of high-quality trout streams in New Zealand is amazing. Many of the lesser-known ones receive little fishing pressure.

TROUT TACKLE

Five-weight tackle serves as a good all-around choice for fly-fishing in New Zealand rivers, though a lighter outfit may be advantageous on small, quiet streams, and stouter gear will be a better option when casting big flies on large rivers. Since I prefer dry-fly fishing, a floating line handled all of my fly-fishing situations. However those who like to cast nymphs and streamers will find some type of sink-tip line helpful.

The Kiwis have definite opinions about leaders. Most insist on using leaders at least 12 feet long, and 16-footers aren't uncommon. The reason: New Zealand's trout are large, wise and wary, and are easy to put down with an errant cast. Still, I had no trouble hooking fish and getting drag-free floats with leaders 11 to 12 feet long. On some small streams 9- and 10-footers worked fine. To handle a variety of fishing situations, leaders should include tippet sizes ranging from 4X to 7X. Shorter and heavier leaders can be used for subsurface fishing with nymphs and streamers.

Flies should include a variety of dries, nymphs, streamers and terrestrials. Traditionally hackled dry flies like the Adams, Humpy, Blue Dun and Royal Wulff are favorites, but I prefer no-hackle flies such as Compara Duns and Sparkle Duns when fish are feeding on the surface, especially in moderate to slow-moving currents. The Pheasant Tail, Hare's Ear, Copper and Prince are among the most productive nymph patterns. Favorite streamers include Matukas, Woolly Buggers and the Red Setter, a locally tied fly. A beetle imitation will sometimes work when all else fails. Most of the same flies that I use in the streams of the western United States work equally well in New Zealand.

New Zealand's browns and rainbows are known not only for their wariness, but for their large average size as well.

from any number of other Kiwi trout streams: plenty of big browns and rainbows, scenic backdrops and clean, sparkling water. But the fact that it is "typical" is part of what makes New Zealand a trout angler's paradise — there are so many waters from which to choose. And like all those streams, the Waipa has little nuances that give it individuality.

The Waipa is a tributary of the larger Waikato River, which connects to Grey's revered Lake Taupo. I guess it could be said that I was still technically fishing in his footsteps, albeit many miles upstream. The medium-sized river is a series of long, deep pools interconnected by short, sparkling riffles. Browns and 'bows are easy to see in the transparent water, but they are difficult to approach in the unhurried and barely discernible currents. To spot fish, Peter and I walked along the high ridges that follow the meandering stream. From those vantage points, we would also develop a strategy to make a presentation to each fish, including where each cast would go and what fly would be used. We spent a lot of time climbing up and down steep banks while tediously making our way from one pool to another through the thick bush.

After catching one or two fish in each of the first few holes, we moved farther downstream to a long bend where various currents converged to form an especially large pool with a massive log jam in the middle. From our promontory we could see trout cruising and feeding; the largest concentration and the biggest fish were centered near the logs. We decided to split up, with Peter taking the tail of the enormous pool and me at the head.

A few feet out from a deep-cut bank just in front of some submerged trees, three big rainbows were intermittently sipping insects off the surface of a swirling current at the top of the pool. From my position about 60 feet away, I could see that the insects were moderately dark-colored mayflies — maybe size 16. Looking through my fly box, I decided on a dark-olive sparkle dun, which I quickly fastened onto the 6X tippet. The best presentation looked to be downstream, so I positioned myself above the feeding fish and made a serpentine cast that landed sufficiently short of the trout so that the fly would drift into their window before the leader came into view. A 7-pound rainbow rose slowly from the depths, ate the fly and quickly broke me off in the logs only seconds after I raised the rod to set the hook. There was no stopping the trout with the light tippet. Sitting down on the bank to re-rig, I watched as Peter went through an almost identical scenario. We waved to each other as he, too, sat down in the shade of some silver ferns to repair his leader and tie on another fly.

I promptly broke off another large rainbow on the new tippet, but Peter successfully landed his next fish, despite the unusually deep bend in his fly rod. Laying my rod and reel carefully on the grassy bank, I grabbed a net and walked several hundred feet to slip the fat 'bow through the wooden hoop and into the twine mesh. As Peter removed the hook for a quick release, I marveled out loud at how much pressure he had used to pull the iridescent fish away from the submerged structure without breaking the leader. "Four-X," he said with a grin, as he handed me the tippet section with the fly still attached. After that single word of advice, my percentage of big fish landed went up significantly, although the resulting increased number of refusals left me somewhat frustrated.

During the next several days, Peter introduced me to a wide variety of North Island waters, a mixture of large, small and moderately sized streams that flowed through hills and meadows with currents that varied from swift-moving to incredibly quiet. Regardless of their differences, they all had several things in common — beautiful surroundings, seclusion and, of course, excellent trout fishing.

Even in my earliest childhood, I can remember my dad telling stories about his times of R&R in New Zealand while serving his country in various World War II campaigns throughout the South Pacific. His tales were fascinating and always included plenty of proud Maoris, friendly Kiwis and flocks of sheep feeding on rolling green hills. It was my hope to someday visit there and realize the visions he had conjured up in my mind. Rarely are such high expectations exceeded, but in this case North Island more than lived up to the images Dad portrayed.

What stood out most was the genuine congeniality of the Kiwis and their willingness to go out of their way to be helpful and courteous. Looking for some good food, nearby lodging or assistance in locating a fishing spot? Ask a Kiwi. Got a question? Ask a Kiwi. Want to fish on private property? Ask the Kiwi landowner. The rest of the world could learn from the wonderfully contagious Kiwi attitude. It's even better than the fishing.

Both large and small streams flow through hills and meadows on North Island, with currents that vary from swift-moving to those that are incredibly quiet.

PLANNING A TRIP

Outside the cost of airfare, a fly-fishing trip to New Zealand needn't be expensive if a visitor is willing to forego a costly lodge with experienced guides and fine dining. Great fishing awaits the budget-minded, do-it-yourself fly-fisher armed with a map, rental car and a sense of adventure. There's no shortage of inexpensive lodging either, including hotels, motels, bed-and-breakfasts and campsites. Restaurants are plentiful and vary greatly in price.

When I was younger, I used to eat most of my meals at convenience stores while driving to and from fishing spots. I often threatened to write the *Gourmet's Guide to Convenience Store Dining*. Well, New Zealand is the convenience-store diner's nirvana — it has a variety of different foods at cheapo prices. A cardiologist might call it the "heart attack special," but hearty meat pies and homemade pastries washed down with Steinlagers are a tasty way to keep the hunger pangs away for most of the day. I'm not sure Zane Grey would have approved, but life is a journey, the enjoyment of which needn't be determined by the size of one's bank account. Sometimes the greatest pleasures are derived from the simplest things.

An excellent source of information for both freshwater and saltwater fly-fishing is Tisdall's, in Auckland. This outfitter can also make arrangements with a guide, including Peter Scott, for anglers who prefer a more directed trip.

Anyone who wants to try the outstanding saltwater fly-fishing around the Cavallis will be hard-pressed to beat the first-class accommodations, beautiful setting and outstanding fishing offered at the Kingfish Lodge. Owner Eb Leery and his staff can also arrange for private saltwater fly-fishing charters and island drop-offs.

Visiting fly-fishers may want to visit a native Maori settlement or watch a rugby (called "football" by the Kiwis) match, especially if the New Zealand Blacks, the powerful national team, is playing. The island country has some outstanding national parks and volcanic regions that are also interesting.

CHAPTER 11

BAJA:
Where the Desert Meets the Sea

A school of racing, leaping dolphin seem to me the very spirit of the ocean personified...
— *A. J. McClane*, Game Fish of North America, *1984*

As our boat began to slow down, richly colored predawn light reflected off the calm Sea of Cortez and painted a deep crimson on the dry and forbidding Sierra de la Giganta Mountain range to the west. Ramon, our guide, eased the 20-foot panga to the edge of a small patch of floating sargassum weed and began tossing live sardines over the side of the skiff even before it had come to a complete halt. Streaks of gold, blue and emerald charged from beneath the seaweed and slashed at the small fish landing on the water. In seconds, John Randolph and I had cast our lines and were skipping saltwater poppers through the commotion. The colorful streaks identified themselves when they struck our flies and simultaneously leaped into the air — a pair of dolphin, known in most Spanish-speaking countries as dorado.

My fly line made an audible hissing sound as it sliced through the water every time the beautiful fish made a short 30-yard dash between soaring leaps. Ten minutes of pumping and reeling brought the dolphin alongside the panga. The sea's broken surface distorted the fish's outline so that it appeared to be a flowing stream of vibrant colors — like some abstract painting. Reaching into the cool briny water, I grabbed the brightly hued acrobat by the tail and held it up for John to see, but he still had his hands full.

For the next several hours, Ramon took us from one frenzied school of dolphin to another. By noon we were exhausted from the severe August heat and the frantic fishing activity. John and I were so damned hot that we had not only sucked all the moisture from each of the 15 or so soft-

drink bottles now lying in the fish box, but we had eaten every bit of ice as well. To hell with what they say about not drinking the water in Mexico. At that moment we would have gladly risked a case of Montezuma's revenge for another swig of the questionable stuff. We were just about ready to fight over who got to lick the bottom of the cooler when Ramon fired up the outboard and headed back to the small coastal village of Loreto for more cold drinks and a well-deserved siesta. That's the way it is in Baja. The heat can be just as intense as the fishing.

Except for the occasional oasis, the Baja Peninsula is a vast desert that extends approximately 800 miles from Tijuana in the north to the southernmost tip at Los Cabos. Only 150 miles wide at its widest point and 30 at its narrowest, the peninsula is home to a mixture of sand, tall cacti, poisonous snakes, ancient Joshua trees, branchless trunks of the ciro and towering mountains, some over 10,000 feet high. But Baja is more than just a desert. It's also a paradox. The dry, desolate landscape is virtually surrounded by water as it separates two great seas teeming with fish — the Pacific Ocean and the Gulf of California (often called the Sea of Cortez).

Both the inshore and offshore fisheries in Baja are extraordinary. Marlin, yellowfin tuna, yellowtail and sailfish roam the blue offshore currents during their respective seasons, while roosterfish, black snook and corvina dominate closer to shore. Over the years, I've enjoyed fly-fishing for each of those species, but when someone mentions Baja to me, the first picture that comes to mind is that of casting flies to schools of dolphin on the still Sea of Cortez in midsummer's hellish inferno.

Baja has long been known for its great fishing. In earlier times though, only the rich and famous could readily access the peninsula in their private planes and yachts. But with the completion of the Transpeninsular Highway and the construction of airports in a few key towns, the fishing has become increasingly available to ordinary anglers. Mulege, East Cape, Los Cabos (including Cabo San Lucas and

Baja California

Loreto

La Paz

Cabo San Lucas

Desert sand and cactus border the edge of the bountiful Sea of Cortez, where a fleet of pangas await anglers for the next morning of dolphin fishing.

CHAYITO

Lucero

DORADO GEAR

Gearing up for dolphin is pretty straightforward. As an all-around choice, stick with a 10-weight rod matched to a reel that holds about 250 yards of 30-pound backing. A full-length fly line will work fine on the average fish, but a shooting-head system offers several advantages. It's great for distance casting with big flies in the wind, and the relatively thin running line reduces line drag on a hooked fish. This system also proves less fatiguing when casting for long periods of time.

Two shooting-head rigs — one with a floating head and the other with a fast-sinking version — will handle any situation for dolphin in the Sea of Cortez. The floating line is indispensable for fishing with topwater poppers, while the sinking line will better handle streamers fished near the surface or well below it. The fast-sinking line is especially helpful when big bull dolphin are the target. The large bulls sometimes hold underneath small schooling fish, and the sinking line often offers the only way to get the fly down to the bigger fish.

Any good selection of dolphin flies should include Ethafoam popping bugs, Clouser Minnows and Lefty's Deceivers tied on hook sizes 2 to 4/0. Bright flies with any combination of white, hot pink, yellow, chartreuse and green will provide sufficient variety. A 50-pound-test monofilament shock tippet will protect light class tippets from the abrasive effects of the dolphin's small teeth.

Ten-weight tackle is ideal for school-sized dolphin. Most any fly will work at one time or another, though popping bugs, Clousers and Deceivers are hard to beat.

San Jose del Cabo) and La Paz are among the few sport-fishing centers scattered along the eastern coast. While they all offer outstanding fishing, the summer concentrations of dolphin offshore from the village of Loreto are exceptional. During the peak of the run, dolphin are so plentiful that they can be seen chasing bait and free-jumping across the horizon. Flocks of seabirds gather above the dolphin as they attack small finfish on the surface.

Commonly referred to as "mahimahi" in Hawaii and most restaurants, dolphin (*Coryphaena hippurus*) are found in warm-water seas throughout the world. It is one of the most iridescently colored fish in saltwater, with a blue-speckled gold body that changes to emerald and then blue again at the dorsal fin. Photographs rarely do the fish justice as they immediately lose their bright hues as soon as they are removed from the water.

Although mature male and female fish have similar coloration, they are easily distinguished from one another. The male, or bull, dolphin has a blunt forehead, while that of the female, or cow, is rounded. Immature fish of both sexes also have rounded heads. Dolphin grow at an incred-

ible rate, weighing about 13 pounds within the first year. Males grow larger than females, with the biggest bulls exceeding 80 pounds in rare instances. They live four to five years. The Sea of Cortez is known as much for the size of its fish as it is for its large population, and several world records have come from its waters over the years. While the average dolphin may be 10 to 15 pounds, in Baja you'll catch fish regularly topping 40.

Dolphin frequently gather in large schools on the edges of current rips and beneath rafts of seaweed, buoys and other floating objects. Their schooling tendencies are so strong that if a hooked dolphin is kept in the water, the rest of the school will remain long enough for a number of the fish to be caught before they become disinterested or swim away. The dolphin's affinity for flies, along with its strong schooling instincts, exciting aerial display and inclination to swim near the surface, makes it the ideal pelagic to pursue with fly tackle.

What's even more impressive to fly-fishers is the tremendous speed dolphin possess. In one of the most incredible displays I've ever seen any fish make, a fly-hooked, 60-pound dolphin performed countless greyhounding leaps in a seemingly unstoppable run that would have done justice to any marlin. Nevertheless, average-sized dolphin aren't known for such long sustained runs, but they do make amazingly high-speed sprints between leaps.

On the Baja Peninsula, the day starts early when dolphin are the quarry, normally well before dawn. That's when the guides go out and gather bait, usually sardines, to use as live chum. Sometimes it takes a half-hour or so, and on other occasions it can last well over an hour. A café con leche can help pass the time when bait is hard to find.

Finding dolphin in the Sea of Cortez is relatively easy for the hard-working Mexican guides, but not all of them are practiced in accommodating fly-fishers. Although the same bait-and-switch procedure used to tease billfish up to the boat transom can also be used effectively for dolphin, it isn't necessary. A good guide familiar with the idiosyncrasies of working with fly-fishers will toss live sardines around weed lines, flotsam, jetsam or other likely looking spots. If fish are present, one or two dolphin will grab the sardines as they try to escape. When a school is found, the competition for the next batch of live chum thrown into the water can create a feeding frenzy — the whole group of fish may attack the bait as soon as it hits the surface. I've seen dolphin so intent on getting to the sardines that they would actually follow the path of the bait sailing through the air. I often wonder how the dolphin avoid a head-on collision with each other, but they all seem to escape unscathed. Obviously, a fly cast into the fray will draw an instantaneous strike.

An alternative method some guides employ involves trolling with lures or bait until a dorado is hooked. The panga will then stop and leave the hooked fish in the water to attract and keep the rest of the school within easy fly-casting range. Although this technique isn't as consistently productive or exciting as chumming with live sardines, it does provide plenty of opportunities to catch fish that congregate around their schoolmate.

Both the "chumming" and "trolling" teasing techniques put more emphasis on a fly-fisher's casting ability than the bait-and-switch method, where a 10-foot flop cast behind the boat transom can lead to success. Since dolphin will frequently follow a fly for some distance before deciding to strike, a longer cast also provides the valuable time that can make the difference between a "looker" and a "hooker."

A school of eager dolphin can turn off as easily as it turns on. The fishing commotion may spook them, or they may lose their urge to feed. You'll see this happen when fish begin to only follow a fly that just minutes earlier seemed irresistible to them. Modifying some part of the fishing procedure can often renew the fish's interest. Try pitching more live chum to the dolphin to generate more excitement, or make a radical deviation from the fly pattern you've been using — from a large topwater popper

to a small streamer, for instance. I always take along two fly-fishing outfits, each rigged with a drastically different fly, for just such occasions.

Dolphin inhabit the Sea of Cortez year round, but early summer through late fall is the peak period. Water temperatures are at their warmest then, and the dolphin arrive in great numbers. As an added benefit, seas are much calmer then than at other times of the year. The placid seas allow fly-fishers to access the fishery via the smaller, inexpensive pangas, where cooler months usually require bigger and more costly cruisers.

Even though dolphin are prolific breeders and have a rapid growth rate, I recommend practicing catch-and-release unless you'll be keeping a fresh fish for dinner. "Tailing" is the easiest way to boat small to medium-sized fish with the least amount of damage. Handling larger fish is often a two-man operation requiring one hand under the operculum at the lower jaw and the other hand on the tail. Lip-gaffing is another viable alternative. No matter what method you choose, keep a tight grip because a "tired" dolphin can still possess an amazing amount of strength. Of course, the same could be said about a hot, thirsty angler suddenly faced with a green-and-yellow blur behind his fly.

Dolphin are strikingly beautiful saltwater game fish, but their color fades almost immediately after they're removed from the water. Below: Watering holes are a welcome sight at the end of a day in Baja's torrid summer heat.

PLANNING A TRIP

Loreto is a small coastal oasis about halfway down the Baja Peninsula. Over the years, commercial jet service to its airport has been interrupted from time to time because of a lack of tourists. That's good in a way because it means Loreto isn't yet on the list of Baja's expensive *chichi* destinations. Aero California currently has regular flights from Los Angeles.

The Oasis Hotel has long been a mainstay for visiting anglers. The charming hotel offers quiet dining and comfortable rooms to anglers seeking solitude. Those who require more amenities can stay at the newer El Presidente, which offers first-class accommodations, including pool, bars, restaurants and even a disco. Both hotels can make charter-boat arrangements, but there's certainly no assurance that the guide will know how to work with fly-fishers. Some self-acknowledged "fly-fishing" guides end up taking their clients out to troll flies behind the boat. Fly-fishermen can avoid such hassles by booking through one of the many established travel agents that specialize in Baja fishing trips.

Burro alert! Travelling any distance at night is not recommended. Gravel and dirt roads are usually bumpy, narrow and winding and often have blind corners. Accidents are common. In addition, burros have a habit of standing in the roads at night, and vehicles I've travelled in have barely missed hitting them on several occasions. If you must travel at night, sit in the back seat. It's safer — unless the vehicle rolls off some precipice, of course.

CHAPTER 12

PAHAYOKEE:
Snook in Florida's Last Frontier

There are no other Everglades in the world. The mangrove becomes a solid barrier there, which by its strong, arched roots collects the sweepage of the fresh water and the salt and holds back the parent sea. The supple branches, the oily green leaves, set up a barrier against the winds, although the hurricanes prevail easily against them. There the fresh water meets the incoming salt, and is lost.

— *Marjory Stoneman Douglas,*
The Everglades: River of Grass, 1947

Although it was dawn, the sun had not yet emerged over the distant tree-lined hammock to the east. The annoying hum of the electric trolling motor was completely out of place against a background of bird songs, mullet splashes and the all too frequent buzz of hungry mosquitoes. My brother Paul and I were casting our flies against the thick mangrove-lined shore of one of the 10,000 or so islands that make up a great portion of Everglades National Park.

A dead mangrove snag at the end of a small tidal creek looked promising. Its bleached remains lay in about 4 feet of brackish water where it had fallen years before, perhaps the victim of some previous tropical disturbance. Overhead, lush vegetation created a shady canopy over the wooden carcass, and a diversity of small marine creatures passed through its branches, pushed by the ebbing current.

At first glance, we were unable to distinguish the dark, shadowy figure of a large fish camouflaged by the arboreal surroundings of the lifeless tree. But on closer inspection, we began to make out the fish's bronze sides, gleaming brightly in the sunlight whenever it ambushed prey swept along in the falling tide, and a prominent lateral line was highly visible as it fed. Snook!

I moved the small skiff quietly into position, and Paul made a mend cast slightly up-current of the fish to give the fly time to sink and drift naturally with the current. We watched the streamer glide and twitch as Paul manipulated the line. When the fly approached the snook's lair, the fish flashed and the fly disappeared. Paul tightened up on the line and then swung the rod sharply to the side, planting the hook firmly in the fish's mouth. Simultaneously, I began backing the boat away from the deadfall.

The snook's natural instinct was to make a powerful surge for the submerged tangle of dead mangrove branches, but Paul's quickness, rod angle and firmness on the line stopped the fish before it could enter the structure. Unable to overcome the unyielding pressure, the snook came thrashing to the surface and then turned for open water. Once it swam away from the underwater obstruction, Paul had a distinct advantage even though the fish continued to put up a tremendous fight. As the length of the runs shortened, Paul eventually brought the weary fish alongside the boat, where he grasped the lower lip, removed the streamer and returned the snook to the tannin-colored domain over which it presides.

There are several species of snook, but by far the most sought after and widely distributed is *Centropomus unidecimalis,* or common snook. Depending on geographic location, it's also known as robalo, linesides and saltwater pike. The species ranges in tropical and subtropical coastal waters from Florida and southwestern Texas to Brazil. South Florida, particularly Everglades National Park and the surrounding area known as the "Ten Thousand Islands," has the best snook fishing in the United States.

As near as anyone can tell, the term "glade" is derived from an old English word that describes an open grassy place, but Native Americans more descriptively called the region Pahayokee, or Grassy Water. Ten Thousand Islands is a group of mangrove islands that border the mainland Glades via a massive and pristine estuary of interconnected bays, sloughs, coastal rivers, sawgrass swamps, marshes and mangrove

Florida

Naples

Everglades National Park • Miami

Florida Keys

In the Ten Thousand Islands, tangled mangrove roots represent prime habitat for snook, especially on a falling tide. The alligator, famous icon of the Everglades, is a common sight in the River of Grass.

Holding a snook by the lower jaw paralyzes the fish, allowing easy hook removal. The snook's thick lateral line has earned the fish its "linesides" nickname.

shorelines. This maze of waterways and bits of densely vegetated land forms the perfect habitat for snook.

Like all estuaries, the Everglades is a place where freshwater and seawater environments converge to form a most diverse ecosystem. The percentages of fresh water and salt water within the estuary depend on the tidal flow, wind speed and direction, river current and rain runoff. Strong river currents, plentiful runoff, falling tide and onshore winds favor an influx of fresh water into the backcountry. Conversely, strong, sustained offshore winds, rising tide and little rainfall increase the salinity. While the glades are also home to tarpon, redfish, seatrout, snapper, sharks, jack crevalle, and even largemouth bass and bream in its upper freshwater reaches, this environment is clearly the snook's domain.

Snook are "euryhaline," which means they can withstand wide variations in water salinity levels. Although usually found in salt water or brackish waters of the glades, they occasionally migrate inland far into fresh water. But these fish are considerably less tolerant of temperature. Sudden drops in temperature from cold fronts can shock the snook and even cause death. Preferred temperatures range between 72 and 86 degrees; they cannot endure water below 60 degrees.

In Florida, the fish concentrate along the coast, at the mouths of tidal rivers and in the passes between barrier islands during the warm months of late spring, summer and early fall. As the weather cools, many fish begin to migrate into the interior creeks and rivers of the backcountry where they can be found throughout the winter. When temperatures begin to warm in early spring, snook will often converge along dark, shallow mudbanks that act as solar collectors to warm the fish after the cold weather. May through August is prime time to fly-fish, but snook are readily available in the Everglades year round. Fish in the 5- to 15-pound class are common, but some may top 35 pounds.

Like largemouth bass, snook like to station themselves around structure

GLADES GEAR

Fly tackle for snook must be sturdy: 8-, 9- and 10-weight outfits will put adequate pressure on fish heading for cover and will prove sufficient for casting large flies even when it's windy. I regularly carry two fly rods for snook in the Everglades and Ten Thousand Islands — a long one and a short one. In almost all situations, I prefer an 8 1/2 - or 9-foot rod, but in extremely tight confines where there's a low mangrove canopy over a narrow tidal creek or cove, a short rod about 6 feet long can be invaluable. After some experimentation, I found that a short 8-weight "bushwhacker" rod can be made from a progressive-action spinning rod blank normally designed to cast 1/4- to 3/4-ounce lures. In some instances, a fly-fisher can achieve almost the same effect of a small rod by choking up on a long rod. But in the most demanding situations the short rod will handle better.

Floating lines will adequately tackle most snook-fishing situations in the Glades, but a sink-tip or intermediate line is a better choice for deep water. In open areas where there is plenty of room to cast, I normally choose a standard weight-forward fly line that is correctly matched to the rod. But in close quarters where casts are consistently under 30 feet, I recommend using a saltwater taper at least one weight heavier than designated on the rod. That's because line designations are based on the weight, in grains, of the first 30 feet of a fly line. For every 2 1/2 feet you cast below that 30 feet, you effectively reduce the line weight roughly by one designation. For instance, if you're consistently loading the rod with approximately 27 1/2 feet of an 8-weight line, you're casting the equivalent of a 7-weight line. A heavier line, like a 9-weight, will compensate for the shortened cast and allow the rod to load faster.

and edges, including deep cuts, deadfalls, docks, potholes, points of land, eddies, shoreline pockets, surf, canals, drainage ditches, tidal passes, seawalls, bridges, jetties, drop-offs and oyster bars. All these exist within the greater Ten Thousand Islands/Everglades area, but the mangrove jungle is where the snook is king. That's because the mangrove's pneumatophores, or root system, is the source of a rich food chain that supports not only a healthy population of snook but also numerous other game fish. In addition to the myriad of small sea animals that live within the relative safety of the mangrove's entwined tentacles, the roots offer limitless places from which the snook can attack prey, and the mangrove canopy provides shady protection from the harsh sub-tropical sun. But the mangroves are also host to hordes of mosquitoes, and fly-fishers should be prepared for the inevitable swarm of the hungry critters.

Proper presentation is vital when snook-fishing in the Everglades. Snook will usually take a stationary position that faces into the tidal current to spot prey the ebb and flow of water sweeps to them. Generally speaking, flies should either be presented as if swimming along naturally with the tide or pulled away from a fish's location like fleeing quarry.

Because thick jungle covers most of the Glades and Ten Thousand Islands, accurate casts must often be made far back under low, overhanging vegetation and around other obstacles where it looks almost impossible to present a fly. Sidearm casts and tight loops are an absolute necessity around mangroves, where a fly must frequently be "skipped" into the tightest spots. If you don't get hung up from time to time, you're probably not casting close enough to the target. A snook won't venture far from protective cover to take a fly, so a few inches can make the difference between success and failure. Once the fly has been worked about 15 feet or so away from the target, pick it up and recast.

On the flats surrounding the Ten Thousand Islands, snook can be even more wary than when hanging in the mangroves. Long casts are frequently needed, especially as the water surface becomes increasingly calm. Look for the fish to be lying in potholes scattered about the grassy flats.

Snook also inhabit tidal cuts and passes where water is exchanged between open bays and the sea. As the deluge of water from these open expanses converges into a narrower passage, snook will position themselves at the discharge end of the funnel to ambush the abundant small marine life carried by the

current. The discharge end changes with each shift of the tide. A presentation should be quartered up-current of the fish's location and stripped as the fly and line are transported down with the flow of water.

Tide and light conditions play major roles in the snook's diverse feeding habits. In the Everglades, snook prefer a strong tidal flow regardless of the tidal phase, and water movement is frequently strongest within the three days before and after new and full moons. A falling tide is generally considered best because it forces the small finfish, shrimp and crabs out of the refuge of high-water hiding places, such as mangrove roots, and into open water where they become easy prey. Nevertheless, incoming water also provides excellent fishing. Snook prefer to feed at night or during periods of low light, but anglers fishing during the day can usually find more than their share of hungry customers.

The snook's most distinguishing characteristic is a long, dark lateral line that runs the length of its body from the gill cover to the tail. Each scale

Sturdy tackle will help combat the snook's strong first run back into its mangrove lair.

The maze of twisting tidal creeks, hidden bays and submerged oyster bars of the Everglades' backcountry are a fly-fisher's paradise, but a navigational nightmare to the unfamiliar. Along the way you'll undoubtedly see a variety of bird life, including plenty of wood storks (below).

© BARRY AND CATHY BECK

in the lateral line system is connected to a large nerve leading to the inner ear. This highly sensitive system is able to detect small movements and sounds — an essential asset in the Glades' dark tannin waters. As a result, flies that make noise, push water and have a lot of action are often the most effective. However, a heightened sense of hearing also requires that anglers approach them quietly.

Fly-fishers should also note the snook's protruding lower jaw and high eye position, traits that are typical of fish that normally feed on prey stationed at the same level or above. Flies should be chosen with these feeding characteristics in mind.

Snook are opportunistic feeders and will readily strike a variety of sub-surface streamers and top-water popping bugs in sizes 2 to 3/0. Some personal favorites include spun deer-hair sliders, Lefty's Deceivers, Clouser Minnows, bend-backs, Seaducers and my own Wobblers and

Rattlin' Minnows. I have a real penchant for topwater flies not necessarily for their ability to produce fish, but because they provide the added excitement of seeing one of the most explosive surface strikes of any saltwater game fish. Although color isn't particularly important in fly selection, light colors seem to work best in clear water, and darker patterns are good choices in more opaque water. Monafilament or wire weed guards will help reduce entanglements in the thick cover that snook frequent.

Short, powerful bursts of speed and thrashing jumps are the snook's trademark fighting qualities. A fish can come up behind a fly, strike and head for structure with such quickness that a careless angler will barely have time to raise the rod before the line is wrapped around some underwater obstruction. At times, a snook can seem virtually unstoppable when it makes a strong run to cover, meaning that a fly-fisher sometimes has to risk breaking the tippet by keeping a grip on the line to avoid entanglement. Frequent break-offs are just part of the game.

Once caught, snook require careful handling. Although they don't have sharp teeth like many other marine fish, their gill covers are extremely sharp and can severely damage a hand that gets behind them. To avoid serious cuts, always pick up snook by grasping the lower lip and jaw — much like you would a largemouth bass. This handling technique not only substantially reduces the chances of injury, but also renders the snook immobile so that a fly can easily be removed before the fish is released.

The snook and its Everglades environment constantly challenge a fly-fisher's skills. Difficult casting situations are the norm, and the snook's unyielding fight can test even the most experienced angler. Hungry mosquitoes, pesky no-see-ums and hot, sultry weather can add to the frustration. But for those willing to accept the demands, the reward is catching one of salt water's premier game fish in a highly unique ecosystem. "There are no other Everglades in the world."

PLANNING A TRIP

Even with proper charts and a GPS, navigating the most remote areas of Ten Thousand Islands is not for the inexperienced. A few days with a professional guide can be a real benefit not only in getting around in the backcountry, but also in learning the intricacies of fishing the area as well. Fly-fishers familiar with the complicated network of waterways can use johnboats, canoes, sea kayaks and small skiffs.

U.S. Highway 41, also known as the Tamiami Trail, bisects the Everglades between Miami and Naples. While driving on the trail, it's easy to understand how Marjory Stoneman Douglas decided on the title of her now classic book *The Everglades: River of Grass*. Great savannas of sawgrass stand above the shiny sheet of water that flows slowly to the south. This is the home of the alligator, Florida panther and wild orchid. More important to fly-fishers, the brackish waters close to the highway are home to snook and a variety of other freshwater and saltwater fishes.

Even though fly-fishers can stay at any number of inns along the Tamiami Trail, the tiny enclaves of Flamingo, Everglades City and Chokoloskee offer the best opportunities to get the full Everglades experience. All three are situated within the River of Grass and Ten Thousand Islands, but each is unique. Here are a few of my favorite places:

Everglades City comes as close to "old Florida" as possible in the urban sprawl of south Florida. The village was originally named "Everglades" before Barron Collier purchased almost all the landholdings in 1922 to create his own personal town. Among these purchases was the home of George W. Storter Jr., who used his waterfront home as a lodge for sportsmen interested in the excellent hunting and fishing that Ten Thousand Islands and the Glades had to offer. Collier expanded Storter's place and renamed it the Everglades Rod and Gun Club. The rustic lodge is still operating today, and it's a wonderfully interesting throwback to a bygone era.

Just a short distance up the Barron River is the Barron River Marina. Its diverse accommodations include small rooms, nicely appointed mobile homes and small individual houses built on stilts.

Across the bay from Everglades City is Chokoloskee Island, a small outpost built on the remains of an old Calusa shell mound. The island's long and fascinating history is a conglomeration of hermits, Native Americans, bootleg liquor, drug running, fishing, poaching and plume hunters. Because of its proximity to the north end of Everglades National Park, I generally prefer Chokoloskee Island over Everglades City. That's not always possible, though, because the island has fewer places to stay. My favorite is Outdoor Resorts, an RV park that rents motel rooms and fully furnished travel trailers in addition to its RV sites.

Flamingo rests at the southernmost tip of the Florida Peninsula near Cape Sable. Commercial fishermen and hunters once inhabited the area, but today it hosts the Everglades National Park headquarters, including a visitor's center, restaurant, campground, marina and motel that overlook Florida Bay. Anglers can take their catch into the restaurant, where it will be prepared to order. Nature lovers will love Flamingo's remoteness as well as exploring the Everglades' various ecosystems along the canoe and hiking trails.

CHAPTER 13

BELIZE:
Permit Capital

What is emphatic in angling is made so by the long silences — the unproductive periods. For the ardent fisherman, progress is toward the kinds of fishing that are never productive in the sense of the blood riots of the hunting-and-fishing periodicals. Their illusions of continuous action evoke for him, finally, a condition of utter, mortuary boredom. No form of fishing offers such elaborate silences as fly-fishing for permit. The most successful permit fly-fisherman in the world has very few catches to describe to you. Yet there is considerable agreement that taking a permit on a fly is the extreme experience of the sport.
— Thomas McGuane, "The Longest Silence" essay from
An Outside Chance, *1980*

I've always heard that bad things come in threes. If that were the case, I was in for some real trouble. Fishing had been good up to now — lots of bonefish, permit and tarpon — but my luck appeared to be changing. I'd been up most of the night in a storm. The crudely made cabana I was staying in had leaned, shaken and groaned on its wooden stilts throughout the darkness under the strong howling winds, and the floor of my cabana was covered with water from the intense, almost horizontal, tropical rains. Even my bed was damp.

The wind and rains had subsided significantly by the time I prepared to go to breakfast, but then the stilts on the dining hall I was in began to shudder as I was eating my *huevos rancheros* and drinking the strong Belizean coffee. Had the storm returned?

"Earthquake" was the last word I heard as I wobbled down the moving stairs from the hall to the relative safety of the open beach. Being from Florida, the tropical storm didn't bother me that much; I'd been through them before. And I don't mind standing in a boat in heavy seas that pitch and roll. After all, I'm an angler.

But we Floridians aren't used to the earth moving, and since this was my first earthquake I didn't like it one bit. According to the radio a few minutes later, the epicenter was in Honduras only a short distance away. My mind began to quickly calculate the time it would take a tsunami, or tidal wave, to travel to the tiny, flat island I was on. I'm not good at doing math in my head, but by my calculations the exact time was "not long."

After finishing my coffee, I apprehensively loaded the skiff with rods and flies for another day's fishing on the flats. Despite the remaining nasty weather, my guide told me we would be able to find fish in the lee of one of the area's many islands. He was right. Shortly thereafter I had a permit beside the boat, and as I released the smooth and exquisitely rounded fish, my thoughts were far from the possibility of the third disaster. Instead, I was suddenly focused on catching the remaining second and third legs of a flats grand slam — a tarpon and a bonefish. After all, here in Belize it's not always bad things that come in threes.

Belize, known as British Honduras before gaining independence, is a small country on the southern end of the Yucatán peninsula between Mexico to the north and Guatemala in the south. It is a beautifully unspoiled land with dense jungle and the Mayan Mountains running through its center. Mayan ruins, many still undiscovered, stand as testimony to the area's significance in the civilization's pre-Columbian empire. It is the land of five cats — jaguar, oscelot, jaguarundi, margay and puma — as well as innumerable varieties of unique and colorful birds. Just offshore, a magnificent 175-mile-long barrier reef runs the length of the country.

Between the Belizean mainland and the reef is an archipelago of hundreds of mangrove-lined cays surrounded by elongated grass and coral flats that border deep-water basins. This unique habitat, combined with the area's brilliantly clear water, form the perfect environment

Ambergris
Caye

Belize City

Belize

Dangriga

Placentia

Punta Gorda

Belize is noted for its long, narrow flats that drop abruptly into deep water, the perfect habitat for the highly prized permit.

Good numbers of tarpon can be found throughout Belize, but the area around Ambergris Caye has some of the biggest.

© NEAL & LINDA ROGERS

for large concentrations of bonefish, tarpon and permit. The flats offer arguably the world's best opportunity to catch a flats grand slam with a fly rod, and under normal conditions a fly-fisher can expect numerous shots at all three fish during a day of angling. But while I enjoy casting to and catching the bonefish and tarpon, it's the permit that fascinate me the most. They're what keep me coming back to Belize.

The permit is the most difficult of the grand slam species to catch, and some suggest it's the toughest catch on fly tackle, period. The fish is notorious for refusing to eat flies that are perfectly presented, and trying to catch a permit can be as exasperating as it is challenging. There are no certainties.

A permit's instincts are so well defined that describing the fish is difficult without resorting to anthropomorphic terms like "smart" and "cunning." Where bonefish may spook at the slightest noise or movement, permit seem to possess an almost sixth sense that they mysteriously use to detect something amiss. I've even seen the fish roll slightly to one side with an eye looking in my direction, as if to get a better view of me.

Belize holds a tremendous concentration of permit; I've never seen anything like it anywhere else in the world. Like the fish in Ascension Bay, Belize's permit usually are smaller than those in the Florida Keys. They average perhaps 5 to 15 pounds, though fish over 30 pounds could swim right by your bow at any moment. Fishing pressure is light here, especially between Dangriga and Placentia, where noted permit fanatics Winston Moore and Will Bauer regularly pursue their obsession.

Tides play a significant role in the permit's movement and habits. That's especially true in Belize where many of the flats are long and narrow with steep drop-offs on either side, unlike the broad, expansive shallows of other locales. In the hour or two before and after low tide, there's barely enough water to cover the flats, and the fish usually disappear into the adjacent depths. At low tide, the flats are almost devoid of the fish, except, possibly, for a few scattered potholes and the farthest edges of the shallows bordering deep water. Those fish that remain in the skinny water usually move quickly and feed only sporadically, if at all.

On the flats, the permit's diet consists mainly of crustaceans, sea urchins, mollusks and, to a lesser degree, small fish. Favorite crustaceans are crabs and shrimp. To consistently take these fish, anglers must match this "hatch." Crab imitations in sizes 1 and 2 probably make the best

Any selection of flies for a flats grand slam in Belize should include a Cockroach, Bauer wool crab and Crazy Charlies in both weighted and unweighted versions.

choice. In Belize, I prefer wool-bodied styles over those tied with deer hair, yarn and other materials because they look more realistic. Any selection of crab patterns should include a mix of off-white, tan, brown and olive. A few years ago, Bauer discovered that mantis shrimp occurred in substantial numbers in Belize and made up a large part of the fish's forage base. He developed an effective pattern that imitates the mantis, and a

COMPLETING THE SLAM

Fly-fishers looking to keep their lines tight or wanting to complete a grand slam can usually find plenty of cooperative bonefish and tarpon to keep them busy in between permit.

Of the three fish that make up the flats grand slam, bonefish are by far the most prolific on Belize's flats. They're also the easiest to catch. Because the bonefish often congregate in the same places daily, many of the best spots are well-known to local guides and receive most of the fishing pressure.

The average Belize bone weighs around 3 pounds, while anything over 6 pounds is generally considered a large specimen. The small fish often gather in vast schools of flickering tails as they grub along the bottom for various prey. By carefully casting just outside the edges of the school, it is possible to catch a straggler or entice a fish away from the main group without spooking all of them. Sometimes several fish can be caught before the whole school becomes frightened and leaves the area. Larger bonefish usually tail and cruise in small groups, pairs or alone. I have yet to see a bonefish that topped 10 pounds in these waters.

For bonefish, stick with 6-, 7- or 8-weight tackle combined with a floating line and a reel that holds about 150 yards of backing. Crazy Charlies and Gotchas in sizes 4 and 6 should be the mainstays of any bonefish fly selection. Ten-foot leaders tapered to an 8- to 10-pound tippet are standard.

Although the average tarpon in Belize is somewhat smaller than its counterpart in such well-known spots of Florida, Costa Rica and Honduras, there are exceptions, particularly around Ambergris Caye, where silver kings can exceed 100 pounds. In most other parts of the country, 20- to 50-pounders are the norm. Anglers usually take the biggest fish while sight fishing from small "panga" boats.

The tarpon are most plentiful from spring through the middle of autumn. My best fishing has been in summer when the beautiful silver fish gather to feed voraciously on schools of pilchards, or "sprat," as locals call them. Shiny sprat imitations are irresistible to these tarpon, but Keys-style tarpon flies, especially the Cockroach, also take their share of fish. I rely on 10-weight gear and a floating line for most of my tarpon fishing on the flats, but I also keep an intermediate "slime line" on hand for fish in deep water. Standard tarpon reel and leaders complete the outfit.

Small, eager bonefish are prolific on Belize flats. The Blue Horizon Lodge (right) features rustic cabins situated at the very heart of Belize's best permit fishing.

number of fly-fishers now use these successfully. Rust and olive are popular colors. Nevertheless, crab patterns still represent the most productive flies by far, day in and day out.

When it comes to crab fly presentation, anglers follow two basic theories. One method is to lead the fish by only a few feet; the other is to hit 'em on the head. I usually opt to lead the fish just slightly, but if they repeatedly refuse to eat, putting the fly right in front of them can suddenly attract their interest. While leading the fish becomes increasingly necessary in calm waters, the latter method is most effective when wind and wave action disturb the surface.

Regardless of how you make the presentation, to remove any slack line you must "tighten-up" on the crab imitation as soon as it hits the water. Otherwise a permit may ingest and spit the fly so quickly that a fly-fisher may never know the fish took it. The generally accepted stripping technique is to move the fake crab slightly until the fish turns toward it. Immediately after the permit shows interest, stripping should stop, and the fly should be allowed to settle to the bottom like a live crab trying to hide from a predator. Hopefully, the permit will tail as it pauses to pick the imitation off the bottom. Use a strip-strike to set the hook. That way, if you miss the hookup, the crab fly will appear to be fleeing, and the permit may continue to show interest. Raising the rod is an ineffective way to get a hook to penetrate a permit's tough, rubbery mouth and will immediately scare any fish that isn't hooked.

Anyone lucky enough to have hooked a permit is amazed by the fish's tremendous strength and stamina, regardless of its size. The initial run can be incredibly fast and long, sometimes exceeding 150 yards in a few seconds. Hooked fish never speed away from the angler in a straight line. Instead they instinctively swim at angles that wrap line around the coral, sea fans and other underwater obstructions so abundant on Belize flats. Break-offs are also common along the rocky edges of nearby drop-offs. Frequently, the fish will pause at the end of a run to rub their mouths on the hard bottom to disengage the fly. A high rod angle will help reduce the chances of a cutoff. Whenever possible, I also follow the fish to close the distance between us and the number of available obstructions, as well as to reduce the severity of the angle.

Nine-weight tackle matched to a floating line is ideal for permit in Belize, but an 8 is also a good choice. Some fly-fishers prefer 10-weight tackle, though I feel that's a little heavy under normal circumstances. Regardless of line weight, I always keep two outfits rigged and ready in case a fly gets hung up in the coral or grass and can't be extricated without spooking fish. If that happens, I have the guide hold the fouled tackle while I use the backup gear. Reels should hold about 200 to 250 yards of 30-pound backing.

Leaders should be long enough to give a gentle presentation, yet sufficiently heavy to turn over large, wind-resistant permit flies. I use 10-foot leaders tapered to a tippet of between 15- and 20-pound-test. Nicks and cuts are common problems on the sharp coral bottom, so have plenty of leaders on hand.

Any visit to Belize should include a tour of ancient Mayan ruins or a side trip into the Cockscomb Mountain Range.

PLANNING A TRIP

Belize offers some great flats fishing along its coast. Here are a few of my favorites places.

Ambergris Caye: Some of Belize's biggest tarpon can be found on the flats around Ambergris Caye. As a result, guides and their fly-fishing clients on a quest for the plentiful silver kings sometimes overlook the area's populations of permit and bonefish. Nevertheless, the guides are more than willing to find bones and permit for those with more varied interests. Offshore charters for sails and other pelagics are also available, but I'm not aware of any that cater to fly-fishers. Ambergris Caye has a lot to offer to fly-fishers and nonanglers alike. The barrier reef, about a quarter-mile offshore, is one of the top diving spots in the world. Mayan ruins, sea kayaking, shopping and beachcombing may also interest visitors. I highly recommend staying at Journey's End, a full-service beachside resort that has beautiful cabanas, a great tiki bar and some of the finest dining in the Caribbean.

Placentia: Want a grand slam? This may be the best place in the world. If it isn't, it's a close second to Ascension Bay. I've never seen more willing tarpon, bonefish and permit. The flats are gorgeous, and sometimes I find myself mesmerized by the coral and tropical fish when I should be scouting the water for game fish. Bonefish, permit and tarpon run about average size for the Yucatán. Several excellent guides work out of Placentia, although some are considerably less capable. Book ahead with a reputable agent to avoid problems. Ecotours into the mountainous rain forest, diving, sea kayaking and beachcombing are other attractions. For inexpensive, clean beachfront quarters, the thatch cabanas at Green Turtle Inn are hard to beat.

Hopkins/Dangriga Area: The barrier islands immediately adjacent to the Hopkins/Dangriga area may be the permit capital of the world. Nearby flats are loaded with permit, some exceeding 30 pounds. You'll find plenty of tarpon and bones, too, but they're considered secondary citizens to the abundant permit. On a tiny island about a half-hour's boat ride from the town of Hopkins, in the middle of this shallow-water fly-fishing paradise, sits the Blue Horizon Lodge. Owned by native Belizean and legendary permit guide Lincoln Westby, this lodge is a no-frills camp that caters to the true permit enthusiast. Bauer and Moore are mainstays. The few rustic cabins on the island have only basic amenities. There's no air conditioning and no glass in the windows. Meals are simple but nourishing. If you're looking for fine dining and a wine list, go someplace else. But if permit are your passion, look no further.

CHAPTER 14

HANNIBAL BANKS:
Extreme Fly-Fishing

Perhaps the strangest and strongest of the Lutianids (snappers) is the mullet snapper. I don't think they reach as great weight as many of the others that go over 100 pounds, but having caught quite a few of them I do think that this is the best fighter, pound for pound, in the family — and that is saying a lot.

— *Joe Brooks*, Salt Water Game Fishing, 1968

The day was full of surprises for me and my fishing partner, Chet Young. To start with, the sky was so dark and the weather so severe that our small plane had to make an unscheduled landing at a Costa Rican banana plantation. The lightning and torrential rain were nonstop. Nevertheless, we resumed our flight into the turbulence when, according to the pilot, there was a "break in the weather." Chet and I sat quietly during the remaining portion of an extremely rugged ride to the small coastal town of Golfito.

Upon our arrival, we boarded the 115-foot vessel *Coral Star* for a week of fly-fishing at the Hannibal Banks, situated approximately 50 miles off Panama's Pacific Coast. The *Coral Star* was to serve as a mothership, or base of operations, while we fished from smaller sport-fishing boats that were to meet us at the banks. Although the weather still looked exceedingly ominous, Chet and I couldn't wait to cast our flies to the many species of pelagic fish that gather in the area.

That night we watched as both wind and waves increased dramatically. Although we didn't know it at the time, the *Coral Star* was making its way through a tropical depression that was to become Hurricane Gordon just a day later. Throughout the night and midmorning, the seaworthiness of the *Coral Star* was tested to its fullest as the boat pitched, rolled and crashed relentlessly toward our destination. Sleep was next to impossible as I was continuously tossed from my bed, and only the sounds of breaking dishes and banging furni-

ture could be heard above the rhythmic impact of the hull into the powerful waves.

I've always had a fascination with nature's raw elements, and over the years I had often commented, "If I knew I could survive, I would like to experience the fury of a hurricane from a boat." There's an old saying that warns to be careful what you wish for because it just might come true. Those words kept echoing in my head as I made silent promises to myself over the next few hours. The night was long, but by late morning the storm had dissipated and the sea began to settle. It was time to fish. The promises were quickly forgotten.

The Hannibal Banks consist of a series of huge rocky pinnacles, or humps, that project from a depth of 2,000 feet to the surface of the Pacific Ocean. These rugged outcroppings provide ideal habitat for a variety of fish, large and small. Among the largest pelagics: sailfish, marlin, dolphin, wahoo and yellowfin tuna. Inshore along the reefs, you'll find rainbow runner, several types of jack and a variety of snapper. Anglers have barely scratched the surface of this region, and the few commercial fishermen who work in these waters mainly use hook and line. The combination of prime habitat and low fishing pressure has created an exceptional and rare fishery. Consequently, steady action is the norm.

Even in the rough seas following the severe weather, Chet and I enjoyed some excellent blue-water fly-fishing. We landed yellowfin tuna up to 50 pounds and hooked a couple that weighed close to 100. Schools of dolphin surrounded almost every weed line, floating log and flotsam patch we saw. Many of the fish were big — 40 pounds or more — and Chet boated one bull that was almost 60 pounds and a world record on fly tackle. Although we didn't find as many sailfish on this trip as I'd encountered on other trips to nearby waters, the area is known for its excellent billfishing and we did raise a few.

While the blue-water fishery is outstanding, Hannibal Banks offers another unique and excit-

PANAMA CITY

Panama

Hannibal Banks

A combination of low fishing pressure and ideal habitat at Hannibal Banks has created an exceptional fishery.

ing angling opportunity — an ultimate combination of fly-fishing and nature's raw power. Seemingly inaccessible pockets of big fish await the fly-fisher and crew willing to forego the dangers of towering waves breaking against the area's many huge, rocky outcroppings. Casting to and catching these fish amid a surging torrent of seawater is highly challenging and difficult to beat for fly-fishing excitement. But it's not for the fainthearted.

Since one miscalculation can have potentially disastrous results, anglers must have a competent helmsman and seaworthy boat to fish among these rocks with their massive rolling breakers. Capt. Bobby

McGuinness, a local expert, is extremely adept at negotiating around these treacherous areas in his 31-foot sport-fisherman. Between each wave, Bobbie skillfully maneuvered the boat within fly-casting distance while the mate cast a hookless topwater plug to a rock. The surface commotion of the teaser bait instantly attracted the attention of so many big snapper — Pacific cubera and mullet varieties — that the water in the immediate vicinity of the plug turned crimson. The huge snapper voraciously chased and attacked the bait in a piranhalike frenzy. Almost all the snapper, regardless of species, weighed more than 20 pounds, and some easily topped 50 pounds.

Sinking shooting heads are indispensable for making long casts amid cresting waves and strong currents. Note the mate (left) using spinning gear and a hookless plug to tease Pacific cubera and mullet snapper (bottom) from the rocks.

This extreme fly-fishing not only requires a team effort, but also puts demands on an individual's skill and concentration. Casting expertise, fighting techniques and even the ability to maintain balance in a rocking boat are all put to the ultimate test. Any problems and inadequacies quickly become magnified.

Once snapper are teased within casting range, the angler has only a few seconds to deliver the fly. Since the fish will not move more than a few feet from the teaser bait or venture far from the safety of their submerged home, the fly must be presented accurately and with a minimum of false casting. Although casting distance varies from rock to rock, more often than not you'll need a long cast to be in the action. Also, it's important to present the fly correctly the first time fish appear within fly-casting range. If you miss that opportunity, subsequent casts of the teaser plug generally yield significantly fewer fish.

Getting snapper to chase a chugger plug requires little skill or finesse. When the plug lands on the water, the mate simply "pops" or "chugs" it a few times to attract attention. After spotting the bait, the snapper immediately light up, and it becomes virtually impossible for the mate to reel in the plug too

quickly once the fish show interest. Consequently, the snapper will strike any well-presented fly with a vengeance.

These big snappers are virtually unstoppable when hooked. Their inital run is a fast and extremely powerful surge back into the rocks. Anglers lose many fish to breaks and cutoffs within the leader system. Fly lines also get severed occasionally on the rough and jagged edges of rock. A heavy tippet, tight drag, maximum rod pressure and some angling luck are needed to stop these fish with any degree of consistency. The rod must be strong enough to apply intense pressure on a fish headed toward the rocks, yet it should allow anglers to make long casts for extended periods. Anything from a "stiff" 10- to a "soft" 12-weight is a good choice.

Quick line pickup often means the difference between success and failure when trying to stop a big snapper. Fly-fishers should consider using a large-arbor reel or one with a large-diameter spool to increase retrieval rate. A reel capable of holding 250 yards of 30-pound test Dacron backing should be more than enough to handle the run of any large snapper. It will also provide added insurance in case of an incidental encounter with a sailfish, dolphin, wahoo or tuna that often shows up in the

After the tropical storm, outstanding fly-fishing at the Hannibal Banks was the pot of gold at the end of this rainbow. The offshore fishery produced some incredible catches, like this 60-pound dolphin.

immediate vicinity. Fly-fishers can also expect plenty of action from rainbow runner, a variety of jacks and even an occasional roosterfish.

A shooting head with monofilament running line has several advantages over a full-length fly line. A shooting-head system provides the extra distance often needed to reach fish, and the shooting head is easier and less costly to change if lost in the sharp rocks. Finally, the relatively small diameter of a monofilament running line offers less resistance and drag in the surging water than a standard line. For the same reason, I prefer the thin diameter of a fast-sinking shooting head to that of thicker floating or slow-sinking ones. Minimal line drag gets you in closer contact with a snapper, a necessity if you hope to stop its run to the rocks.

Leaders should be short and strong. Typical big game-style leaders with a class tippet section of 20-pound monofilament work best. A short wire shock tippet will negate the effects of the snappers' sharp teeth, especially the formidable caninelike ones of the Pacific cubera snapper.

Rocky edges and sharp teeth also account for a lot of lost and damaged flies at the Hannibal Banks, so it pays to bring plenty of durable patterns. Deer-hair and wool-head baitfish imitations tied on 2/0 and 3/0 hooks are the most consistent producers, but any large and fully dressed streamer will take fish.

All equipment should be corrosion-resistant to withstand the inevitable heavy salt spray that comes from fly-fishing in this heavy surf. A large waterproof container and various sizes of zip-lock bags prove indispensable for storing items susceptible to the corrosive atmosphere.

Fly-fishing has often been referred to as a "merging of art and nature." But in the wild surf that crashes on the rugged reefs of the Hannibal Banks, art and nature collide to extend the limits of fly-fishing far beyond the gentle pastime of Izaak Walton. This is fly-fishing at its extreme.

PLANNING A TRIP

Because of its distance from the mainland of Central America, one of the most practical ways to fish the Hannibal Banks is aboard a luxurious mothership like the *Coral Star*. Such vessels offer conveniences such as panoramic picture windows, wet bar, sun deck, large lounge area, ship's library, movies, finely prepared meals and private sleeping quarters. Those who prefer land-based accommodations can choose to utilize the services of a traditional lodge, usually only a short boat trip away.

Except for fishing, you'll find little else to do at the Hannibal Banks. But that's as it should be in a location with an extraordinary fishery, spectacular rocky shorelines, deep blue water and thunderous crashing surf. Fly-fishing there is a memorable experience — even without a tropical storm.

CHAPTER 15

SLOUGH:
The Cut and the President

It is good to realize that if love and peace can prevail on earth, and if we can teach our children to honor nature's gifts, the joys and beauties of the outdoors will be here forever.
— *President Jimmy Carter,* An Outdoor Journal:
Adventures and Reflections, *1988*

Slough Creek may be my favorite trout stream in the world. I say "possibly" because there are so many wonderful cold trout waters that it is impossible for me to favor one above all others. However, Slough has to be at or near the top of the list for several reasons. My brother Paul and I have countless memories of wonderful fly-fishing and fraternal moments along its banks. Memories filled with intimate conversations and silent understandings mixed with beautiful caramel-colored cutthroats, prismatically hued rainbows and hybrid "cutbows" with the distinguishing marks of both pure-bred species. All this we experienced against a pristine backdrop of a shining meadow stream that flows on the edge of the rugged Beartooth Mountains at the northwest quadrant of Yellowstone Park. With little effort, I can recall the evergreen smell, feel the pull of the current, see bolts of lightning shredding the sky as a storm passes, and hear the harmonious evening howl of coyotes echoing across the valley as I lie alone with my thoughts in the intimacy of a tiny, nylon tent. Slough has always been special.

I have returned to its banks for nearly 25 years and have watched it grow from relative obscurity to one of Yellowstone's jewels. But as Slough's popularity has grown, I have increasingly sought the farthest sections of the creek. One such excursion led me to the upper meadows near its headwaters. The trout were feeding selectively on pale morning duns and emergers, caddis and occasionally the hapless grasshopper or beetle blown into the water by the brisk August wind. It was one of those rare days when everything seemed to come

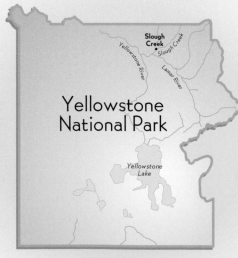

together: the fly, the cast, the drift, the rise and, finally, the take. The fishing couldn't have been better.

I had seen a husband and wife much farther upstream earlier in the day, but had lost track of them as I focused on feeding trout. Infrequently, I paused to enjoy the contrasting scenery of the golden meadow set against dark, jagged mountains and noticed that the number of hikers had increased significantly over the previous year — the presumed result of the area's growing celebrity status.

While working one of my favorite runs, an anonymous, slightly Southern drawl came from my right on the opposite bank. To paraphrase: "I was admiring your cast. Any luck?"

The compliment made me feel good. I assumed that it must be one of the pair of anglers I had seen earlier. "Thanks. Fishing's been pretty good. How are things upstream?" I replied as a cut rose deliberately to take my fly at the tail of the run.

"We got a few on hoppers, but not as many as you seem to be catching. What are you using?"

"The last few rose to a PMD, although they seem to intermittently prefer a small caddis. Haven't tried a hopper yet, but there seem to be plenty around," I replied, never looking up at my anonymous visitor.

Conversation continued as I concentrated on landing the large and vividly colored fish. Finally, as I prepared to release the gorgeous cut, the voice stood before me on the high bank and I caught a glimpse of a famous, toothy 'possum grin. "Jimmy Carter," I awkwardly acknowledged out loud, then more appropriately, "President Carter." Is that what you call an ex-president? It suddenly dawned on me that the "hikers" were probably Secret Service personnel who, by now, had the cross hairs of a riflescope situated on the bridge of my nose.

I had admired Jimmy Carter as governor of Georgia and was a supporter throughout his pres-

The magnificent
Lower Falls is
one of many
breathtaking sights
a fly-fisher will see
in Yellowstone
National Park. I
can't guarantee an
ex-president.

A typical Slough Creek cutthroat in full regalia — bright crimson slash and caramel-colored flanks.

idency. His love for the natural environment and his setting aside more public lands for protection than any other president, including Teddy Roosevelt, were what always impressed me the most. The fact that he and Rosalyn later became avid fly-fishers further added to my respect.

President Carter immediately put me at ease with his sincerity and kindness. We talked at the edge of the creek for quite some time about Slough, Habitat for Humanity and the environment. But mostly we talked about fly-fishing: fish, flies, rods, reels and line. Since Rosalyn had long since headed back to a nearby cabin, he asked me to join him on his way through the meadow. As we slowly walked along the gravel bars and sod banks casting our flies to the small rings left by hungry, rising cuts, I couldn't help but think about the beautiful locations and wonderful people I've come to know through fly-fishing. Jimmy Carter and I shared an attachment to the same remarkable stream and a mutual passion for the act of casting flies. It was yet another memorable day at Slough.

It is appropriate that the unspoiled streams that meander and roar through Yellowstone are home to cutthroat trout that seemingly take on the coloration of the great golden canyons and valleys that gave America's first national park its name. From my point of view, they are the most vividly colored of *Salmo clarki*, with huge crimson gashes at the base of the throat that more resemble open wounds than the thin, pale-red slits of some other subspecies. Cutthroats are endemic to the West, but among some elitists they don't garner the same respect that their alien cousins do. While "cuts" sometimes aren't as wary as browns and can't clear the water like leaping rainbows, they are, nonetheless, determined fighters that often rise only to the most appropriate of flies.

Slough Creek becomes a tributary of the Lamar River just above the Lamar's confluence with the Yellowstone River. In most sections, Slough is a traditional pool-run-and-riffle stream that flows through wide-open meadows along most of its length. Except for two short canyons, Slough is readily accessed on foot, but the farthest reaches require a lengthy hike. The most easily reached part is below Slough Creek Campground. Upstream from the campsite lies First Meadows, about a 45-minute hike up a steep trail. Beyond that, the trail flattens into the Second Meadows, a hike of slightly over three hours. Fishing pressure varies with ease of accessibility, but all sections hold plenty of big, vibrantly colored cutthroats.

I generally use 4- or 5-weight tackle for Slough cuts, and stick predominantly to dry flies. I carry a selection of hoppers, beetles, sparkle duns, parachute Adams, comparaduns, thorax duns and elk hair caddis as my primary patterns. Of course, the size and color are matched to the insects on the water. I like leaders 10 feet long or so, with tippets ranging from 3X for the largest flies to 7X for the smallest.

Wildlife encounters are common while fly-fishing in Yellowstone National Park's fabled waters.

Yellowstone National Park is arguably the epicenter of trout fishing in the United States. Many of its waters are also considered among the finest of their kind in the world. While Slough hasn't quite attained that status, it has a rapidly growing group of followers who enjoy casting in its unhurried currents. Among them is a former U.S. president.

PLANNING A TRIP

You'll find a plethora of written material about the wildlife, geysers, scenery and other natural wonders of Yellowstone National Park, so I won't belabor those points here because it would be impossible to cover these exceptional natural wonders adequately in a few sentences. Suffice it to say that any trip to the area should include more than just fly-fishing for trout.

Those who would like to fish Slough and other extraordinary waters in the immediate vicinity should consider staying in the inexpensive Rough Rider Cabins at Roosevelt Lodge, just a short drive from the creek. The cabins are rustic, to say the least, but they are clean and comfortable. A communal shower, with separate stalls, lies a short walk away. A Hamilton Store is next door to the lodge and has groceries, camping supplies and a modicum of fly-fishing supplies. Roosevelt Lodge serves outstanding family-style meals and a chuck-wagon cookout is available through the lodge too. Horseback riding is another possibility.

The Slough Creek Campground offers primitive sites that front a portion of the stream. The camp fills fast, so it pays to get there early for a spot. Backpackers can pitch their tents on designated sites in the remote upper meadows by obtaining a permit through the park service.

Fly-fishers will want to sample some of the park's other great rivers and streams, including the Yellowstone, Madison, Gallatin, Gibbon, Lewis, Lamar, Gardner, Firehole and Soda Butte. Many other waters in Yellowstone offer great fly-fishing as well.

CHAPTER 16

HOMOSASSA:
Land of the Silver Giants

... There were moments of doubt until you have your first big tarpon in the air. Before that you had been quite pleased with a two-pound rainbow. And still are, though the true maniac deserves a tarpon.
— *Jim Harrison, "A Sporting Life" essay from* Silent Seasons, 1988

The click of the trolling motor switch on the poling tower alerted me to the fact that my frequent fishing companion, Steve Letchworth, must have spotted some tarpon. My eyes shifted with the starboard swing of the bow, and the soft morning light reflected brightly off the shiny dorsal fins of several rolling fish. "Happy fish," Steve muttered under his breath with obvious excitement in his voice as he continued using the push pole and trolling motor synergistically to position me for a shot.

To eliminate any last-second doubts, I nervously checked the mono-core line lying at my feet to make sure it was free of any entanglements. A short, quick pull of line from the reel provided reassurance of the proper drag setting. I had been through the same scenario thousands of times. The blood races as the pod of fish approaches, but the heart pounds even harder when one of the monstrous fish follows, eats and then launches itself from the water with the hook embedded securely in its mouth.

It has become an annual ritual. Every year in late spring, my circle of fly-fishing friends and I re-rig our specialized but normally unadorned skiffs with cumbersome transom-mount trolling motors and extra batteries in preparation for another season on Homosassa's famed tarpon flats. Our fly-tying tables grow littered with the remnants of colored hackles used to fashion a variety of tarpon streamers. Small pieces of monofilament are scattered about, the result of countless Bimini twists and Huffnagle knots. Several days a week, we trade trips with one another in our seasonal quest for big silver kings. Like lemmings, we are driven by a commonality of purpose.

The two-hour drive from Florida's east-central coast to its west-central coast usually starts several hours before sunrise and is accompanied by a bag full of miniature chocolate doughnuts and lots of hot black coffee to wash them down. Both always seem to run out almost simultaneously with our arrival at the Bayport boat ramp. Throughout the trip, our conversation and thoughts have been filled with scenes of giant tarpon with flies in their mouths.

Fly-fishing for tarpon is a tough business. Few fish come to the fly even on a good day, and even fewer are caught. Many anglers measure their success by the number of casts made or the fish that are "jumped." For Steve and me, this proves to be another extended, wonderful day on Homosassa's flats, one filled with long casts to pods of huge tarpon and, occasionally, flashing iridescent scales leaping at the end of a bent rod. Finally, as the sun touches the horizon, a great silver king lies a few inches beneath the gunwale of the sleek skiff. We remove a tiny, feathered hook from the gaping mouth, and after a few minutes of resuscitation, the enormous beast moves with renewed energy. Then it slips with surprising gentleness from our arms and glides slowly into the silent blue world. After a celebratory beer and congratulations, Steve brings the engine to life and we silently reflect on the day's events as the skiff slices through the placid surface on the way back to Bayport.

For tarpon anglers, "Homosassa" is a generic reference to the flats that lie between the village of Bayport and the small town of Homosassa to the north. The area is inextricably connected to saltwater fly-fishing history. As early as the 1880s, a Dr. Ferber was drawing enough attention to his fly-fishing exploits around the area to be called the dean of fly-fishermen on the Florida coast by A.W. Dimock in *Florida Enchantments*. Dimock, himself an early visitor to Homosassa, tells of many of his earliest fly-rod experiences in the state in his classic *Book of the Tarpon* (1911). More recently, several world-record tarpon have come from the flats, including Billy Pate's 188-pounder and the new 20-pound tippet record of 202 1/2 pounds for angler Jim Holland Jr. Fish over 100 pounds are the rule

Florida

Homosassa

Tampa

rather than the exception.

Tarpon can show up as early as late April, when the water temperature begins to hover in the mid-70s, and I've seen good numbers of them still roaming the flats well into July. Prime time, though, lasts from the beginning of May through the end of June. But nothing is certain when it comes to these fish. Homosassa's tarpon population can vary greatly from year to year as well as from day to day. Sometimes they show up strong, and on other occasions they're nowhere to be found.

When tarpon do invade Homosassa's flats, they move in irregular patterns. They prove less predictable there than in the Florida Keys, where the fish follow traditional routes dictated largely by bottom contours and anglers stake out those known passageways waiting for them to swim by. In Homosassa, anglers must move often to find the unpredictable tarpon and position themselves for a cast — hence the transom-mounted trolling motors.

Despite the lack of definite traveling routes, Homosassa's fish do seem to follow some basic patterns. Early in the morning the fish will usually first show themselves around Black Rock and the deep parts of the bay just outside the Chassahowitzka River. These are fresh fish that fly lines and slapping boat hulls haven't yet spooked. From there, they usually work their way in a southerly direction to Middle Flat. By early afternoon, pods of tarpon roam around Oklahoma Flats. The flats and rocks just slightly north of Pine Island often prove reliable spots as the day winds down.

Some fly-fishers take a follow-the-fleet approach to finding fish. They look for the congregation of skiffs, especially the ones operated by local guides, and zero in on them in hopes that they have located tarpon, which many times they have. The members of "the fleet" look like they are playing a game of follow-the-leader as they move like a conga line with the lead boats. Moreover, the congestion makes the tarpon exceedingly nervous and wary, especially on weekends when traffic is the heaviest. I generally prefer to stay out of the way on the extreme periphery of the crowd. Even though I may see fewer fish, they usually are less spooky and more willing to eat. Fewer boats will try to move in on a pod of fish that I'm working, as well. Nevertheless, when tarpon concentrate around the fleet, it's hard to resist the temptation to join them.

A guide or specially rigged flats skiff is a necessity for fishing these waters. Anglers who expect to join the concentration of tarpon fanatics by using the outboard on the back of a bow rider with the radio blaring and the kids yelling at the dog to "stop barking," may end up lynched, shot or both — if they make it back to the ramp at all. Quite seriously, though, a push pole at least 22 feet long, transom-mount trolling motors and a silent approach are essential parts of fly-fishing Homosassa. The operator should shut down the outboard engine before he gets within

about a half-mile or so of another working skiff. Then the trolling motors and push pole come into play. Use the same procedure when leaving. Batteries should be fully charged the night before a fishing trip to make sure they last through an entire day of use. In 8 feet of water, there's nothing more tedious or tiring than trying to pole away with dead batteries from the fleet of skiffs.

A word of caution regarding navigation to and from the tarpon grounds. Some areas are veritable minefields with large submerged rocks scattered about that can do some serious hull damage to the unobservant or uninitiated, especially when low-light conditions make it impossible

Homosassa has a long and rich saltwater fly-fishing history. Today most fly-fishermen consider its flats the premier location for pursuing record-sized tarpon.

Jim Holland Jr. poses next to his record 202 ¹/₂-pound mamoo.

for the helmsman to see beneath the surface.

Watching a pod of giant tarpon seemingly materialize from a dark grass bottom onto bright sand in 6 feet of clear water is an amazingly surreal and awe-inspiring sight — even for the most seasoned saltwater flyfisher. Sometimes the long, prehistoric behemoths will gather in a tight nose-to-tail circle, a primordial mating dance called a "daisy chain," then just as suddenly disperse and continue their linear cruise across broad flats. I've seen many veteran fly-fishers so mesmerized by such conditions on their first tarpon trip that they suddenly fell apart when the time came to present a fly. Their casts either fell short, long, late or in the middle of the school, sending them packing. It's something akin to the buck fever that some hunters experience.

Over the years, several techniques have been developed that have significantly increased the percentage of fish landed. Some are now so commonly practiced that they have become cliché, but no discussion of tarpon fishing is complete without a review.

The presentation: I always marvel that a 100-pound-plus tarpon will go out of its way to engulf a 4-inch streamer, but a successful take largely depends on good fly presentation. Tarpon have a lower protruding jaw typical of fish that prefer to feed at the same level or above them in the water column. The ideal cast presents the fly in such a manner that when stripped, it moves away from a fish like fleeing prey. Any fly coming directly toward a tarpon looks unnatural and will spook it. The cast should allow enough time for the fly to sink to or slightly above the depth of the fish.

A relatively slow retrieve draws the most interest, but if a tarpon follows a fly, increasing the stripping speed will often entice it to strike. A fish loses interest whenever the pace of the streamer slows or stops, although some fly-fishers hesitate just slightly before the strike so that the fly gets ingested deeper for a better hookup. On many occasions, I've seen a tarpon follow a fly so closely that the hook appeared to be balanced right on the tip of the upper jaw, like a ball on the nose of a seal. Again, a couple of long, quick pulls on the line may trigger an immediate feeding response. If after several good presentations the tarpon show no interest, it's time to change the fly pattern or color.

Hooking and playing: Once a tarpon eats a fly, the next obstacle becomes getting the hook to penetrate the fish's fabled hard mouth. Traditionally, anglers sharpen standard saltwater hooks by running a metal file unidirectionally from the point to the barb to form cutting edges on either three (triangulated) or four sides (diamond-shaped). Recently, circle hooks have grown popular as well.

Once a fish inhales the fly and then turns away, hold the line firmly with the tip of the rod momentarily pointed at the tarpon to get a good hook-set. Follow this with sideways jabs of the rod at right angles to the fish to further ensure penetration into its bony mouth. When a tarpon begins its powerful run, concentrate on clearing line off the deck by holding the tip of the index finger and thumb together to form a circle through which the line must pass. Tarpon normally jump almost immediately after they feel resistance. Bowing, or dipping, the rod toward an airborne fish reduces line pressure and should happen on every leap to lessen the chances of the hook pulling or the tippet breaking. After the fight begins, the tarpon will tire quickly if the rod remains at right angles to its swimming direction.

Fly rods for tarpon should have powerful butts with good lifting capabilities to move big fish. I normally opt for a 12-weight rod to deal with Homosassa's monsters, but I've even used an 11-weight with success. Many fly-fishers prefer a 13-weight rod, although it's a bit unwieldy for my taste. Reels typically hold about 250 yards of 30-pound Dacron. Big-game-style leaders with an 80-pound monofilament shock tippet are standard. I usually carry along at least two outfits rigged respectively with a monocore intermediate sinking line and a monocore sink-tip. An extra-fast-sinking shooting head can come in handy when probing for tarpon in the deepest holes.

My favorite streamer for tarpon at Homosassa, as well as many other locales, remains a Cockroach. Not so much because it is necessarily the fly, but more because I've developed confidence in it over the years. Still, if the fish seem to show no interest on a particular day, I am more than willing to change. Since it's hard to predict what might interest the fish, just use the eenie-meenie-minie-mo method to pick other Keys- and Apte-style tarpon streamers. That selection process is based on the philosophy that "even a blind dog can find a bone once in a while," and it has worked surprisingly well for me over the years. Regardless of the pattern, I like flies tied on 3/0 and 4/0 hooks.

When the tarpon run ends, my friends and I somewhat regretfully remove the trolling motors and batteries. It is a time of transition. With

During the peak of the tarpon run, fly-fishers may find better fishing on the extreme periphery of the skiff "armada."

© R. VALENTINE ATKINSON

the reduction in weight and the elimination of the transom appendages, the clean skiffs are ready to resume their duties in Florida's truly skinny water, where we target redfish, bonefish and permit. While our focus begins to shift, we can't help but look back at the previous few weeks — the pods of great silver fish and of battles won and lost.

PLANNING A TRIP

Although the region around Homosassa is rapidly growing, the more established neighborhoods still have an old-fashioned Florida look about them. Several of the oldest buildings date back to the time when Dr. Ferber and A.W. Dimock pioneered these waters. Adding to the charm is a picturesque coast bordered by spartina grass marshes. Except for the nuclear power plant to the north that stands as a naked monument to Homer Simpson fans, the area is a nature lover's delight.

Nearby Crystal River (its name indicates the water clarity) offers some great snorkeling and diving with an excellent chance to see a manatee, as well as a variety of fishes and land-based wildlife. Visitors may also want to check out the remnants of an ancient village of Indian mound builders at Crystal River State Archaeological Site on the river's north side. And you'll find some great largemouth bass fishing at Lake Tsala Apopka and on the Withlacoochee a few minutes east of Homosassa. Those who enjoy more manufactured entertainment can catch the mermaid show at Weeki Wachee Springs. My favorite restaurant in the area is Crump's, on the scenic Homosassa River across from McRae's, a waterfront motel and marina that is a base of operation for many fly-fishers.

Many guides operate in these waters, but the best are usually booked far in advance of the tarpon season.

CHAPTER 17

ASCENSION BAY:

Heavenly Fly-Fishing

No one can really tell why a permit hits a fly. You can make a thousand casts to the fish and get a turn-down on every one. Then, you make another cast and the permit charges like a cavalryman.
— Mark Sosin and Lefty Kreh, Fishing the Flats, 1983

The daggerlike caudal fins that suddenly and silently pierced the water's surface were difficult to see amid the last glints of reflected light from a fading sun. Nevertheless, my observant Mayan guide, Javier, whispered in a barely audible voice, "*Palometa, señor, palometa*," and nodded toward a pair of protruding tails that waved back and forth. My Spanish vocabulary is limited to only a few essentials having to do with fishing, eating and finding a bathroom quickly, but *palometa* is near the top of that short list.

About 60 yards away, a pair of permit had momentarily paused to feed on some of the crustaceans that seem to be so prolific on the broad saltwater flats of Mexico's Ascension Bay. Without a sound, I slid from the small skiff to begin an approach that would quickly intercept the fish in the final minutes of what had been an outstanding day of fly-fishing. As I quietly neared the ever-widening ringlets left by the intermittently feeding fish, I began to false-cast, waiting for the permit to reveal themselves again. They didn't. The silent shadows had vanished without a trace.

Even in the waning twilight, I could see Javier's brilliant white teeth grinning at me. We both clearly understood the thrill of the previous few moments. There was no disappointment — quite the contrary. The day had been filled with the excitement of speeding bonefish, leaping tarpon and the grand-slam *pièce de résistance*, the permit. This final failure at the onset of darkness stirred us as much as the successes.

Ascension Bay is approximately 100 miles south of Cancun on Mexico's Yucatán Peninsula. The very word "ascension" implies something heavenly or on a higher plane, and this body of water lives up to its name. Covering more than 50 square miles, the lagoon's unspoiled waters and expansive sand flats provide ideal habitat for bonefish, tarpon and permit. Because of the sizable numbers of each species and the eagerness with which they attack flies, a grand slam remains a strong possibility here. As a matter of fact, Ascension Bay and adjacent lagoons of Boca Paila are among the easiest places, if not the easiest, in the world to accomplish the feat of catching a bone, permit and silver king in a single day's fishing with fly tackle.

The easiest leg of a grand slam is the bonefish. The bay has a huge population of them in the 3-pound range and over the years, I've caught a few that weighed over 6 pounds. Specimens exceeding 7 pounds are rare. The concentration of bonefish varies greatly from one portion of Ascension to another. In some locations the fish are scattered, while in others the bones frequently gather in great schools, creating large "muds" as they feed and move along the sandy flats. Many times, I've been able to take a half-dozen or more fish from such a school by approaching them on foot and making long casts to the periphery so as not to alarm the entire bunch. The smallest fish tend to gather in the heaviest concentrations, often with their protruding tails flickering in the sunlight like a mass of twinkling stars. The biggest fish are more solitary and are often found in pairs and small groups. Although these bones are on average somewhat smaller than the trophy-sized fish of the Florida Keys and some parts of the Bahamas, Ascension Bay fish come more readily to the fly. That means lots of action for those like me, who find the sizzling run of a hooked bonefish to be one of the most exciting events in fly-fishing.

Fly-fishers will find no shortage of permit either, considering the area is one of the premier permit destinations in the world. Anglers catch 5- to 20-pound fish with regularity, and even bigger fish are not uncommon. Ascension may have more trophy-sized fish than other parts of

Isla Mujeres

Cancun

Mérida

Mexico

YUCATÁN PENINSULA

Cozumel

Punta Allen
Ascension Bay

the Caribbean, with some occasionally topping 30 pounds. The permit's feeding habits are much the same as those of the bonefish, rooting in the sand and mud for crustaceans, mollusks, sea urchins and, to a lesser degree, small finfish. When tailing to feed on the bottom, their dark sickle-shaped tails easily distinguish them from the bonefish that frequent many of the same flats. The fish are so prolific in bay waters that I prefer to concentrate solely on them when conditions are just right. While Ascension permit tend to be more aggressive than those in many other hot spots, they are still permit. No other marine fish is more finicky or more challenging to catch with fly tackle. Even when everything is done correctly, a permit will more than likely turn up its nose at the offering and swim off in the opposite direction.

Tarpon are not found in the same great numbers here as either bonefish or permit, but there are some good areas where the fish congregate with regularity, especially when large pods of green-back herring, or "sprat," are nearby. The relatively deep and quiet waters immediately adjacent to mangrove islands offer some of the best fishing for the silver kings. Fly-fishers will also occasionally encounter tarpon while scouting the flats for bones and permit. The tarpon average slightly less than 50 pounds, though I've occasionally seen bigger ones. The tarpon are normally very aggressive and come readily to the fly unless they have been fished by a previous angler, as is sometimes the case late in the day at local hot spots.

Although I don't recommend it, fly-fishers willing to compromise a lit-

Fly-fishers can expect to get plenty of shots at permit during a day's fishing in Ascension Bay, making a grand slam an excellent possibility.

I usually take along a floating line for shallow water as well. Ascension's silver kings have a profound fondness for Keys-style tarpon flies like the Cockroach. However, when pods of green-back herring are plentiful, the tarpon will focus on them as prey and will readily strike a sprat imitation, often to the exclusion of all other flies. Both Keys-style and sprat flies should be used in combination with a standard tarpon leader that has an 80-pound shock tippet.

Although a boat is usually needed to catch tarpon in Ascension's waters, wading can be the most productive and pleasurable way to pursue bonefish and permit. When fish are located, guides will often stop the boat to allow the angler to wade within casting distance. Most of the flats have a sandy bottom that provides firm footing, but neoprene flats booties are essential protection from coral, sand, shell fragments and other sharp and abrasive objects. I would also recommend long pants with elastic bands around each leg to eliminate irritating, but harmless, bites from sea lice, a small crustacean prevalent throughout the bay.

Tidal fluctuation varies greatly from one part of Ascension Bay and its adjoining lagoons to another. Normal tidal exchanges occur in the immediate vicinity of areas connected to the open sea, but in the farthest reaches of the bay system the fluctuations are minimal and, in some cases, nonexistent. When tidal influence is a factor, guides generally prefer incoming water in most places, but some locations are more productive on the ebb. Where the rise and fall of water are restricted, time of day and wind direction can have an increasingly profound effect on fish

Crazy Charlies and Gotchas prove deadly on the eager bonefish that frequently gather in huge schools on Ascension's flats. Look for tarpon (right) in deep, quiet water near mangrove islands.

tle can get by with an 8-weight outfit as an all-around choice for each of Ascension's game fish. I prefer to take at least three fly-fishing outfits along on each trip to the flats — one for each of the grand-slam fish.

While 8-weight gear is generally considered standard for bonefish in many parts of the world, 7-weight tackle is probably better suited to the fishing conditions in Ascension Bay. Even lighter gear can be used when the waters are calm. Reels that hold 150 yards of backing will easily handle the blazing run of any bonefish, and leaders approximately 10 to 12 feet long and tapered down to 8-pound tippet help assure a delicate presentation of lightly weighted flies. Size 6 Crazy Charlies and Gotchas are perfect. I've never needed anything other than a floating fly line.

A 9-weight rod matched to a reel that holds 200 yards of backing and a floating line proves ideal for permit. Orvis' Redfish Taper Fly Line, with its short front taper and heavy belly, is a superb choice for casting the heavy, wind-resistant crab patterns that are so effective on the fish. Bonefish, Tarpon and Saltwater Taper Lines also perform well. Ten-foot-long leaders with thick butt sections tapered down to a tippet of around 16-pound test or heavier will assure adequate, yet relatively gentle, turnover.

While the same rod and reel used for permit can double as an outfit for the average tarpon, 10-weight tackle is a better choice. An intermediate line works well in the deeper water that tarpon normally prefer, but

© BARRY AND CATHY BECK

Ascension Bay lies within the Sian Ka'an Reserve, a remarkable 3,000-square-mile ecosystem consisting of dense jungle, clear bay waters and mangrove-lined islands.

The tiny bayfront village of Punta Allen makes a great base of operations for anglers fishing in Ascension Bay and adjacent waters.

movement, with early morning and late afternoon usually offering the best opportunity to fish.

In addition to a bountiful fishery, some of Ascension Bay's most outstanding characteristics are its seemingly endless number of coves and small islands. These geographical features not only provide plentiful habitat for tarpon, bonefish and permit, but also offer a fly-caster some degree of protection from the wind, regardless of its speed and direction.

Local guides are mostly of Mayan descent. Having fished with many of them over the years, I have found that all are extremely adept at locating and spotting fish. Like most Mayans, they are typically friendly, yet shy. Few of them speak much English, but that's part of the charm of fishing in Ascension. It also gives me time to practice my Spanish, and often our well-intentioned attempts to communicate in each other's language lead to some funny moments that keep us laughing most of the day.

The Yucatán Peninsula was once a hub for early Mayan culture, and

its influence becomes readily apparent to even the most casual observer. Small, unrestored ruins are scattered about the bay's thick jungle shoreline, and the crumbling base of an ancient Mayan road remains clearly visible from the water. When fishing the flats, fly-fishers should watch for *cenotes*, natural freshwater upwellings in the middle of the bay that the Mayan people once used as their source for potable water.

The Mayans referred to Ascencion Bay as Sian Ka'an, which roughly translates into "birthplace of the sky." That's probably a reference to the fact that water and sky here often meld into a monochromatic-blue space in which the horizon is indistinguishable, a scene that is actually quite common on tropical and subtropical waters when conditions are calm and cloudless. The phenomenon gives the illusion that the sky is rising from the water.

Bay waters are situated within the Sian Ka'an Reserve, a remarkable ecosystem that includes over 1 million acres, an area equal to 3,000 square miles, set up by UNESCO to study the interaction between man and natural environments. The unique environment and fascinating history of Ascension Bay and surrounding areas provide a colorful and extraordinary backdrop in which to stalk shallow-water game fish. Anglers regularly share the flats with flocks of flamingos, roseate spoonbills and a variety of other beautiful birds. And if the casts are accurate and the fish are willing, there's always the possibility of a grand slam. Such prospects rank the bay among the best saltwater fly-fishing spots in the world.

Mayan influence is readily apparent throughout the Yucatán Peninsula. The ancient city of Tulúm lies only a short drive from Punta Allen.

PLANNING A TRIP

Getting to Ascension Bay requires flying into the gaudy resort town of Cancun at the extreme tip of the Yucatán Peninsula. Depending on the time of arrival at the airport, some travelers opt to overnight in Cancun. Others continue on the long trip to Punta Allen at the northern end of the bay. The unimproved dirt road to this tiny village is extremely bumpy and either dusty or muddy, depending on the weather. As an alternative to staying in Cancun, I recommend spending the night on the quaint nearby island of Isla Mujeres to enjoy some offshore fly-fishing for sailfish (see chapter 3).

Because of the proximity to Ascension, most fly-fishers stay at one of several lodges near Punta Allen in Quintana Roo Province. Most are situated on beautiful secluded beaches. Anglers looking for quality dining and first-rate accommodations should consider Seaclusion Lodge. Pesca Maya Lodge is an option for those who want to save a few bucks and don't mind slightly less elegant digs. Although less ritzy than Seaclusion or Pesca Maya, Cuzan Guest House offers clean cabanas and good local foods for the budget-minded. All three lodges have friendly and knowledgeable guides and staff.

Remnants of ancient Mayan civilization can be found throughout the Yucatán Peninsula. On the drive to Ascension Bay, visitors can visit the well-preserved Tulúm ruins on the cliffs overlooking the Caribbean Sea. Nearby towns of Chichén-Itzá and Coba also have some magnificent ruins that are well worth a short side trip.

Local foods are not the stereotypical Mexican fare of tacos, burritos and tamales. Because of coastal Yucatán's proximity to the ocean, seafood is used in the majority of its favorite dishes. For a special treat, try the Yucatán version of conch seviche, a blend of fresh peppers, onion, tomatoes, raw conch (a tasty mollusk) and other ingredients simmered overnight in lime juice. The lime juice chemically "cooks" and tenderizes the conch. It's a delicious and refreshing way to end a long day of fishing in typically hot weather. To spice up any meal, select from one of the many delicious hot sauces made from locally grown habañero peppers, but be forewarned: Their reputation as the hottest peppers in the world is well-deserved.

CHAPTER 18

THE DEAN:
Dean of Steelhead Streams

On the Dean again. What would I do without this river? I design my year around this week. I dream of its pools and its beautiful, beautiful fish. Dean fish are always appearing in articles about steelhead fishing. They're just better looking than other steelhead. These are the dream slabs.

— *Thomas McGuane*, Live Water, *1996*

A thick cloudy mist settled in less than 100 feet above the river and shrouded the entire valley in various shades of gray. In this dim achromatic setting, a silver projectile launched itself from the water and then plunged to the depths in a showering spray. My friend Terry Yamagishi had hooked another steelhead, his second one in the past hour. Running line flew from Terry's stripping basket as the big hen shot downriver and jumped again. I was too far away to help, but as I watched him play, land and subsequently release the fresh-run wild steelhead, my thoughts turned back to the many years of outstanding fishing we had enjoyed on one of North America's premier steelhead rivers, the Dean. It was a scene that had replayed itself several times amid the raw splendor of British Columbia's coastal wilderness.

A recent lack of rainfall kept the river clear and the water level relatively low during our stay. Continuous cloud cover created the low-light conditions the steelies prefer and helped assure good fishing throughout each day. Since we were fishing in July near the peak of the run, every high tide brought a new group of bright steel-gray fish into the river. Conditions were near perfect on this quintessential steelhead river, and the fishing was among the most exciting either of us had ever experienced.

Capt. James Vancouver explored the Dean River in 1793 and named it after his Irish friend, Dean James King. Originating at Anahim Lake in the heart of the Coastal Mountain Range in central British Columbia, the remote river has changed little over the past 200 years. The Dean winds

northwest for more than 150 miles through a magnificent wilderness of glaciated mountains and thick conifer forests before merging with the sea at the Dean Channel Fjord. Clean and highly oxygenated water, combined with a riverbed of glacier-crushed gravel, provides ideal habitat for the various spawning anadromous salmonids.

During the summer months, groups of slate-colored steelhead gather at the Dean River's confluence with the fjord to await the tidal surge that will start them on a reproductive pilgrimage back to their freshwater beginnings. The run usually starts in June and continues through September. Some species migrate as far as 50 miles upstream.

According to Mike Ramsay, Fisheries Zone Supervisor for B.C. Environmental, two varieties of steelhead are found in the Dean River — the Takia strain and the Dean River strain. Ramsay says that these summer-run fish are especially strong because higher water temperature during the warm months helps the steelhead conserve energy. The annual run has been estimated at approximately 3,500 fish in recent years. Average weight runs about 12 pounds, with the largest specimens exceeding 25.

When the fish first enter the mouth of the lower portion of the Dean, they are at their strongest, not yet wearied by the forthcoming trip against the river's cold and powerful current. These ocean-bright fish present the ultimate challenge for fly-fishers who seek wild steelhead in a pristine and scenic environment. Consequently, Terry and I decided to concentrate our efforts just above the river mouth where the strength of the fresh-run fish would be at its peak. Many of the fish we caught were such recent arrivals from salt water that they came with sea lice still attached.

As the steelhead make their way upstream, they instinctively take the path of least resistance to help conserve the energy necessary to complete their journey. According to Dean River guide Wayne Taylor, the fish travel mostly in the top 3 feet of the water column and usually during the daylight hours. Along the way, the steelhead will stop

British Columbia

Tweedsmuir
Prov. Park

Dean River

Vancouver
Island

VANCOUVER

British Columbia's
wilderness streams
and rivers provide
the perfect
backdrop for
catching wild
steelhead and other
salmonids.

periodically to rest in pockets and around underwater obstructions such as submerged logs and rocks that reduce the force of the Dean's current. It is only when they are holding at such a suitable resting station that the steelhead are vulnerable to a fly-fisher's offerings. The fish will not strike while on the move, and they avoid water that is either still or extremely shallow, so it pays to concentrate on water that has current and a depth of at least 18 inches. Furthermore, fishing usually proves best when the skies are overcast. Knowing about these migratory patterns and behavior characteristics is essential to productive fly-fishing for steelhead on the Dean.

To efficiently and effectively fish this large and somewhat intimidating river, first identify potential holding water and then use a systematic

A fresh-run Dean River steelhead comes to hand with sea lice still hanging from its belly. Below: Fly-outs can produce a variety of other salmonids like this chum, or dog-toothed, salmon.

ty rather than hunger. Consequently, most strikes come only after a great deal of perseverance and experimentation. I've found that repeated casts to obvious holding spots, as well as to fish sighted in clear shallows, often get the most hookups. In addition, a change in fly pattern or color is sometimes all that's needed to coax a steelhead.

Terry and I typically focused on pools and other holding areas where

GEAR UP FOR STEELHEAD

Because the steelhead season on the Dean partially overlaps with runs of large king and chum, or dog, salmon up to 50 pounds, local guides almost unanimously recommend a 9-weight outfit for all-around fly-fishing on the river. However, I prefer 8-weight tackle when steelhead are the primary target. Pull out the heavier tackle when large salmon are the main focus.

You'll need a broad selection of fly lines in different densities to effectively fish the various depths and current speeds of the Dean. Sink-tip lines and sinking shooting heads with fast and extra-fast sink rates are indispensable for keeping a streamer down in the rapid flow. Even better are the specialty salmon/steelhead lines that weigh close to 300 grains. For dry-fly fishing, you'll find a floating line essential. Short leaders of less than 7 feet are a good match with sinking lines, while a 9-foot leader is a better choice when fishing on the surface. Go with a tippet strength of 10- to 12-pound test. Reels should have enough capacity to hold approximately 150 yards of backing plus fly line.

Submerged rocks and trees, as well as the steelhead themselves, can substantially reduce any angler's inventory of flies. It pays to have a good supply in sizes 6 through 1/0. Favorite streamer patterns of local guides include Purple Peril, Egg-Sucking Leech, Black Wooly Bugger, Skykomish Sunrise, General Practitioner, Squamish Poacher and Purple-Orange-Red Popsicle. I would also add the Muddler, Green Butt Skunk and Boss to that list, but any number of salmon/steelhead streamer flies can be fished effectively on the Dean. In general, bright fluorescent colors are more productive in cloudy water, while dark patterns are a better choice when the water is clear. For dry flies, I prefer Bombers, Humpies, Wulff Patterns, Waller's Waker and the Steelhead Bee.

Summer weather in this part of British Columbia can fluctuate widely within a short time. A morning trip on a jet boat can be a bone-chilling experience for those who aren't prepared, but a lightweight shirt may be quite comfortable in the early afternoon sun. Bring along clothes suitable for high and low temperatures as well as sunny and rainy conditions. Because luggage is limited to 40 pounds per person on Wilderness Airline flights from Vancouver, the most efficient way to adapt to changes in temperature is by using layers of lightweight clothing. A breathable waterproof raincoat will prove invaluable in the frequently wet weather, and a fleece jacket provides added warmth when temperatures drop.

approach to casting. Randomly casting about the water will yield only minimal results. Casts should be made across the current or quartered downstream, and then allowed to swing with the flow of the river until the presentation is directly down-current. Upstream mends will help govern the speed of the drift and give a fly-fisher more control on the strike. In addition, I've found that an occasional twitch of the fly will further entice the fish, particularly at the end of the swing. Try to cover one small section of water by the completion of every drift. Once you've worked an area in this manner, repeat the process slightly downstream.

Since steelhead rarely feed during their trip into fresh water, enticing one to strike can sometimes seem like an exercise in futility. A fish generally takes a fly because of an instinctive aggression or curiosi-

the steelhead might pause during their spawning run. These spots usually contained submerged and partially submerged rocks or logs. Sometimes it can be difficult to tell whether a fly has snagged on some underwater obstruction or been ingested by a steelhead. On several occasions I've seen anglers try to dislodge their fly from an imagined snag only to have the line suddenly slice through the water with a steelhead on the end of it. Usually they lose the fish because they never set the hook. Avoid such a predicament by strip-striking whenever the line hes-

itates. Of course, a sharp hook can also help.

Such fishing challenges only add to the raw splendor of the Dean and its overwhelming surroundings. Powerful currents, radiant ice fields, towering waterfalls, misty fjords, virgin forests and precipitous snow-capped mountains provide the perfect backdrop for anglers who pursue wild summer-run steelhead with a fly. This ultimate combination of outstanding fishing and natural beauty culminates in a magical outdoor experience.

PLANNING A TRIP

Only a limited number of anglers and guides are allowed on the Dean's 40-mile stretch of productive steelhead water at any one time. A drawing is held for fly-fishers hoping to enter the upper end of that stretch, while those who want to fish the lower section can hire a local outfitter with access to it.

The John Blackwell family and employees of Moose Lake Lodge operate the oldest outfitting service on the lower Dean. Situated in the wilderness between the upper Dean and the headwaters of the Blackwater River (often called West Road River on maps), the main lodge at Moose Lake acts as a base of operations from which anglers can take a floatplane to Blackwell's other lodge near the mouth of the lower Dean. There, Dean River Camp offers jet-drive boats, comfortable cabins and wonderful home-cooked meals in a friendly atmosphere. The convenient location at the mouth of the river affords fly-fishers the opportunity to catch steelhead at their strongest — fresh from the sea. Knowledgeable guides help assure a successful trip.

Many of British Columbia's fabulous fisheries are situated close to Moose Lake Lodge. In addition to steelhead fishing on the Dean River, the lodge also arranges fly-outs to the nearby coastal rivers for coho, chum, pink and king salmon, as well as steelhead. Fly-fishers can also cast to healthy populations of rainbow trout, cutthroat trout and Dolly Varden that inhabit the seemingly countless number of lakes, rivers and streams of the region's interior.

At the lodge, small skiffs are available to those who want to catch and release the strong and plentiful Kamloops strain of rainbow trout that reside in Moose Lake. Because peak seasons for salmon, trout and char overlap with the steelhead run, a fly-fisher can catch a wide variety of game fish during a relatively short stay at the lodge. That diversity also assures plenty of fly-fishing action even if rain temporarily creates high-water conditions on the Dean.

CHAPTER 19

COSTA RICA:
Bicoastal Slam

In the midnight Arctic seas, stained tropical rivers at dawn, the Gulf Stream at noon, where thin shafts of light chisel down into blue-black; a small creek in evening shade beneath willows and sycamores; in northern rivers where salmon lie in deep viridian hollows. It is always the dark water which promises most.

— Russell Chatham, Dark Waters, 1988

The ecological relationships that exist where freshwater rivers interact with the sea on the eastern and western shorelines of Costa Rica never cease to amaze me. It's easy to understand how Costa Rica got its name, which translated into English means "rich coast." Actually, rich *coasts* would have been more appropriate as it lies on the edge of both the Caribbean and the Pacific. Costa Rica boasts extensive undeveloped coastlines with an abundance of diverse estuaries that serve as the basis for gigantic and complex food chains. The fisheries on each coast are as distinct as their ecosystems.

On each of my past trips to Costa Rica, I have concentrated my fishing efforts on either the Caribbean side or the Pacific side. That is until my friend Jim DiBerardinis suggested an "ultimate fly-fishing adventure" pursuing four of Costa Rica's most prized game fish: tarpon, snook, sailfish and roosterfish on both coasts. Jim is a part-time Tico, or Costa Rican resident, so he volunteered to schedule the trip when fishing conditions on both coasts would be optimal. He decided on the end of February, well before the rainy season. Although snook fishing might be only slow to fair, fishing for sailfish, tarpon and roosterfish would be near the peak.

East Coast

We were to begin on the Caribbean coast. In contrast to the mountainous terrain that dominates most of the country, the extreme eastern portion is relatively flat, with sand beaches and dark rivers that wind through dense tropical rain forests before merging with the sea. Small finfish provide a plentiful forage base for the ultimate predators — tarpon and snook — that prowl these inshore waters. My fishing experiences on such jungle rivers have been memorable and include plenty of giant tarpon and hard-fighting snook. The Rio Colorado, long considered one of the world's premier fishing destinations for both species, would be the perfect spot to complete the Caribbean side of our trip.

The Rio Colorado is a wide and deceptively fast moving river that originates in the high mountain regions. A number of rare and endangered animals, including tapirs, toucans, crocodiles and jaguars, live within its watershed. Islands of partially submerged logs, thick overhanging vegetation and deep holes scoured out by the current create the consummate backwater environment for snook and tarpon. However, the largest concentrations of these two game fish exist at the river's terminus.

To reach fish in the open sea you must travel through the river mouth, a sometimes treacherous mixture of shallow bars, high waves and strong conflicting currents. Some of the local lodges use flat-bottomed johnboats to navigate the opening, and even with skilled guides, it can be a hair-raising, if not dangerous, experience. We stayed at Silver King Lodge, partly because it provides seaworthy 23-foot V-hull boats to fish in the ocean and Carolina Skiffs for the quiet water of the backcountry. Most importantly, the guides there understand the intricacies of fly-fishing for tarpon and snook. And the Silver King's accommodations are first rate: spacious rooms, excellent food and a screened-in hot tub that is a welcome relief after a day of battling the river's big fish.

During our three days of fishing, we concentrated on schools of tarpon in about 60 feet of water just outside the Rio Colorado's mouth. Once we spotted fish rolling on the surface, our guide would promptly maneuver the boat to drift within casting range, and Jim and I would cast, hoping that tarpon in the school would see and strike our flies. Hookups were consistent

Rio Colorado

Costa Rica

SAN JOSÉ

Drakes Bay

Osa Peninsula

Casting bulky flies with fast-sinking lines along the shoreline of the Rio Colorado can produce snook as well as tarpon.

when we could sight-cast to rolling fish, less so when fish stayed deep and we had to resort to blind-casting. Using a combination of sight fishing and blind-casting, we each jumped four to six fish per day. Most fell in the 80- to 100-pound range, but larger fish are not uncommon.

Fly-fishing for tarpon in deep water outside the river mouth can test both physical and mental strength. It requires a lot of casting with heavy rods matched to extra-fast-sinking shooting heads. Anglers who aren't up to this generally "jig" their flies behind a drifting boat instead of casting for fish. To further complicate the situation, after the initial hookup and a jump or two, a tarpon heads for the depths where a long, arduous tug-of-war ensues. Consequently, tackle selection is critical to comfortable, yet efficient, fly-fishing. Although 13-weight or heavier rods give a decided advantage when trying to move a tarpon in deep water, they can be exhausting to cast with cumbersome sinking lines over extended periods of time, especially when trying to cover lots of water blind-casting. A 12-weight or even a strong 11 is a better choice. These work perfectly in the river as well.

When the water becomes clearer, some tarpon move back into the Rio Colorado and congregate in the deep holes, particularly in "Banana Holes 1, 2 and 3." Those spots were unproductive on our trip, however, because recent rains had roiled the water, but they do offer some outstanding action under the right conditions.

Because the tarpon fishing was so good and peak snook season had passed, Jim and I mostly cast to the silver kings. However, we did spend a few hours skipping flies beneath overhanging trees, probing deep holes and casting long lines near the surf for snook. Both of us managed to catch a few under 10 pounds, but the numbers of fish just weren't there like they are from September to January. During those months, the riverine environment is home to a huge population of common snook, *Centropomus unidecimalis*, that average around 10 pounds and regularly exceed 20. In addition, between November and mid-December the river experiences a run of fat snook, or "calba," that commonly weigh 6 to 8 pounds.

The biggest snook generally hang out in the surf and at the mouth of

Good-sized sailfish, or pez vela, are plentiful in the waters off Drakes Bay along Costa Rica's Pacific coast.

80-pound test for the tarpon and 40-pound for the snook.

At the end of our stay, Jim and I were exhausted from long days of casting to and fighting the big fish of the Colorado. Our knowledgeable guides had kept us in fish, but it was time to fly back into San José, the capital of Costa Rica, before moving on to the west coast for the second part of our adventure.

West Coast

After a good night's rest in San José, Jim and I took a small plane into Palmar, a typically sleepy little Central American town surrounded by large banana plantations. From there, a boat took us along the scenic Sierpe River and across a portion of Drakes Bay to Aguila de Osa, a jewel of an inn on the Osa Peninsula.

National Geographic once called this peninsula the "most biologically intense place on earth." It's also one of the most beautiful. Osa Peninsula is surrounded by towering waterfalls, a lush tropical rain forest, dark jungle rivers and great rocky cliffs and hills that drop off into the unspoiled waters of Drakes Bay at the edge of the Pacific Ocean. Compared with other parts of Costa Rica, the fishery at Drakes Bay remains relatively untapped. Sailfish are plentiful, and the roosterfish action ranks among the best in the world. If it sounds like I'm partial, it's because I am. The area's combination of natural beauty, solitude and outstanding fishing is difficult to beat in the angling world.

We had arranged for accommodations at the Aguila de Osa, an exceptional inn nestled in the rain forest. The inn has 24- and 31-foot charter boats only a few minutes away from outstanding offshore and inshore fishing. More important, the charter-boat crews are cooperative and thoroughly familiar with the teamwork necessary to catch roosters and sails with a fly.

Because they are hard fighting, extremely wary and highly selective when it comes to flies, roosterfish have become one of saltwater fly-fishing's most sought-after prizes. While several Central American countries have outstanding roosterfishing, few areas can compare with the consistent action at Osa Peninsula. In the clean water of a rising tide, great numbers of the fish congregate around the countless submerged rocks that lie only a few hundred feet from the beaches. The incoming water brings various prey for the roosters to feed on.

Fly-fishers can use three methods to catch roosterfish. When fish are near the surface and their distinctive comblike dorsal fins protrude above the surface, sight-casting becomes a viable, albeit relatively ineffectual, option. Blind-casting also yields minimal results and is tiring as well. The most effective technique is trolling with hookless teaser baits and employing a bait-and-switch. When a hot rooster attacks a hookless teaser, the skipper takes the boat out of gear, and the angler makes the cast. Jim and I raised close to 100 roosters and landed almost 30 in our three days of

the Rio Colorado where it joins the Atlantic. The most efficient way to fish these open waters is to prospect with long casts to cover as much area as possible. A 9-weight outfit proves ideal, but a 10-weight will give a little added insurance in case a tarpon decides to grab a fly intended for snook, which sometimes happens. Regardless of the line weight, a shooting-head system with an extra-fast sinking head is ideal when probing for snook just outside the river mouth. The same tackle can also be used to fish for the slightly smaller snook in the river.

Because of limited visibility in the river's murky waters, sparsely dressed, Keys-style tarpon flies are practically useless. Tarpon more easily detect bulky flies that "push" water. Dan Blanton's heavily dressed Whistler flies were designed specifically for such conditions, and they are top producers of tarpon as well as snook. Yellow-black-and-white variations tied with a red collar on hook sizes 3/0 to 5/0 are the most popular. I prefer the bigger sizes for tarpon and reserve the smaller ones for snook. Big-game-style leaders should have a shock tippet of at least

rate of retrieve than anything else. But to my knowledge, there is still no one definitive pattern for roosters. I have had a good deal of success using relatively plain-looking 6-inch streamers tied with sparse amounts of blue, green and white synthetic hair. Use a double-hook setup to catch the reluctant feeders that often hit the rear of the fly.

Because of the outstanding roosterfishing, Jim and I waited until the last few hours of our stay before testing the offshore waters for sailfish, but that was all we needed. Bait was plentiful, and the water had the kind of slight chop that so often precedes good sailfishing. It took only a few minutes to raise, tease and hook our first sailfish of about 100 pounds. In less than three hours, we raised four sails, hooked three and landed two — a fitting close to an outstanding week of fishing!

While Quepos and Flamingo get most of the publicity for Costa Rica's outstanding sailfishing, the relatively untapped fishery at Drakes Bay is every bit as good and possibly better. During the peak period, from December until the beginning of May, anglers frequently land five or more sails per day. Most of the fish top 90 pounds, and specimens weighing more than 120 pounds are caught regularly. Crews use the now classic bait-and-switch technique to get these fish to strike.

Typically large and bulky double-hooked billfish flies are ideal for sailfish. White, blue-and-white, green-and-yellow and pink-and-white are among the most popular colors. I've found that sailfish flies tied with Owner hooks penetrate the fish's extremely hard mouth well.

Whether you're after tarpon, sailfish, snook or roosterfish, few countries can match Costa Rica's outstanding opportunities to catch each of these. But far too many anglers visit only one coast to target just one or two species. With the Pacific and Caribbean shores so close to each other, anglers should consider a bicoastal odyssey of their own to pursue the very best of Costa Rica's inshore and offshore fly-fishing.

fishing with this method. It was the best fly-fishing for roosterfish either of us had ever experienced.

After experimenting with various stripping techniques for roosterfish, I found that a rapid retrieve is essential. A one-handed stripping technique, no matter how proficient, is just too slow to consistently entice this fish into striking. Instead, use a two-handed retrieve with the rod tucked under your casting arm for more hookups. If a fish follows a fly without striking, sweep the rod sideways to speed up the retrieve and possibly get a response. A long cast will help increase your odds, but more often than not, the curious but reluctant roosterfish will refuse your feathered presentation even when performed to perfection. But that's part of the attraction of fly-fishing for roosterfish.

It also has been my experience that roosterfish will usually show a decided preference for one fly over another, based more on size and the

PLANNING A TRIP

Aguila de Osa and Silver King Lodge are two of the finest inns on their respective coasts, and both are situated at the center of some of the most outstanding fly-fishing in Costa Rica. Knowledgeable guides and first-class boats help assure not only a quality fishing trip, but a safe one as well. Both lodges have excellent accommodations and finely prepared foods. Silver King Lodge also has a small tackle store on the premises and keeps an adequate supply of flies, lines, rods and reels on hand. Sea kayaks, diving equipment and hiking trails are pleasant diversions for those staying at Aguila.

One benefit of a bicoastal trip to Costa Rica is that the same tackle used for snook and tarpon on Costa Rica's east coast is also appropriate for fishing the west coast. The 12-weight shooting head system used for tarpon can double as tackle for sails, and the 9-weight shooting head outfit needed for snook is ideal for casting to roosterfish. The leaders used for tarpon and snook will also work well for their respective counterparts.

CHAPTER 20

THE FLORIDA KEYS:
Bonefish Road

Most bonefish must die from ulcers. They feed and swim in a constant state of alarm. Bonefish do not have lockjaw, supersensitive noses or any sort of radar that can pick up an enemy angler a half-mile away, although all of these possibilities may seem reasonable to a bonefisherman at sometime during his career.
— *Lefty Kreh*, Fly Fishing in Salt Waters, 1974

The placid water of Florida Bay blended perfectly into a cloudless sky, and the horizon was lost in a vast blue realm. The melding together of sky and water gave distant mangrove keys the illusion of being suspended in the steamy salt air. The only disturbances in this monochromatic stillness were an occasional passing shorebird and the quivering tails of two bonefish that had paused to grub for food at the base of a small mangrove shoot. Their tails intermittently disappeared and then reappeared somewhere up-current whenever the pair stopped to forage in the sandy bottom.

As the fish continued to work along the flat, I cautiously waded into casting position. The first cast landed 5 feet in front of the feeding bones, but they either ignored the presentation or did not see it. The second cast was almost identical to the first, and this time the lead fish immediately turned and began following the fly, its body visibly trembling as if overcome with the excitement and anticipation of eating some tasty sea creature. After tracking the fly for about 10 feet, the bone suddenly surged forward and stopped with its head down. A slight tug indicated that it had taken the fly. I tightened up on the line, and when the bonefish felt the resistance it raced toward deeper water like a torpedo. To reduce drag on the line and to decrease the chances of a break-off on some underwater obstruction, I instinctively raised the rod in what has become the classic "over-the-head" position. In seconds, the fish was out of sight, but the bright-green line pointed to its location almost 125 yards away.

Strands of turtle grass gathered at the tip of the rod while I slowly collected line back onto the reel. As the spool started to fill, the bone sped away again — this time on a run about half as long as the previous one. After about 10 minutes of this give-and-take battle, the fish was too tired for any more extended bursts of speed and simply began swimming around me in ever-tightening circles. Finally, when the bonefish had fought to the point of almost total exhaustion and could no longer struggle, I slipped a hand under its firm belly, removed the small brown fly and placed the fish back in its shallow sanctuary. Its barred light-green back and mirrored sides immediately blended the 10-pounder in with its surroundings, so much so that I could only follow the shadow of the "ghost" as it swam away and then disappeared altogether.

The very roots of fly-fishing for bonefish began on the flats surrounding the Keys. In an 1896 issue of *Forest and Stream*, an angler using the pen name Maxie claimed to have 10 years of experience fly-fishing for bonefish "using a medium-weight fly rod with large gaudy salmon or bass flies." Nevertheless, noted Keys guide Bill Smith is generally credited with the first "intentional" catch of bonefish in 1939, even though anecdotal written accounts favor Maxie.

The small islands that make up the Florida Keys stretch approximately 150 miles from Miami to Key West and are connected throughout by U.S. Highway 1, often called the "Overseas Highway." Florida Bay parallels the north side of the road, and the Atlantic lies to the south; both bodies of water are clearly visible throughout much of the highway's length.

Fly-fishing opportunities are seemingly endless along the flats, channels and cuts that immediately border the thoroughfare. Bonefishing, in particular, is so good on many of the adjacent flats that I like to refer to U.S. 1 as "Bonefish Road."

The Overseas Highway was completed in 1938. It was originally constructed using the bridges and much of the railroad bed of

Henry Flagler's Florida East Coast Railway, which was extensively damaged in the horrific Labor Day hurricane of 1935 when winds reached an estimated 200 to 250 mph. Once opened, the road brought increasing numbers of sportsmen who were anxious to pursue the island chain's legendary game fish. Today, an improved version of the highway still offers anglers easy access to what remains one of the best saltwater fly-fishing destinations in the world.

My history in the Keys began in the mid 1960s when some college friends and I ventured there for a fishing trip during spring break instead of opting for the popular resort towns of Daytona and Fort Lauderdale. I fell in love with the place immediately and returned at every opportunity until graduation, when I started working as mate on various charter boats in Key West. My goal was to get the experience I needed to operate my own guide service. Over the next several years, much of my spare time was spent cruising the Overseas Highway looking for productive flats. Eventually, my fishing buddies and I found some great spots where we could cast our flies in the Keys' crystal-clear waters and watch silver fish accelerate across the shallows. I still regularly visit many of

The Overseas Highway passes alongside some of the most productive bonefish and permit flats in the Florida Keys.

those same places and fondly remember past experiences.

While bonefish are plentiful throughout the Keys, the flats between Key Biscayne and Big Pine Key have the biggest population. The number declines slightly to the west of Big Pine. Keys bonefish are relatively large, compared with those in many other places, and fish in excess of 10 pounds are somewhat common. However, along with the big size comes an increased wariness that will test a fly-fisher's mettle. These are not the small and eager fish so prevalent in the Caribbean.

Exploration with local charts can yield some great fishing. Fly-fishers can also find productive flats by inquiring at local fly and tackle shops or by hiring a guide for a day or longer to help find quality roadside fishing spots. Many excellent bonefishing flats are pinpointed in *Top Spot Charts* and *The Florida Keys Fishing Charts* available at most of the area's tackle and sporting goods stores. Although long out of print, Stu Apte's booklet *Fishing in The Florida Keys and Flamingo* is another good source that some libraries still have on their shelves.

There are several factors to consider in prospecting for a likely flat. You'll need to start with a good working knowledge of the bonefish's interrelationship with tides, temperature, habitat and prey. Flats alive with rays, barracuda, sharks, snappers and other small fishes may also

Opportunities for roadside fly-fishing are seemingly endless in the Keys. Local tackle stores and charts will usually point to great fishing.

geal teeth at the back of their mouth to crush the shells and carapaces.

Fly patterns for Florida Keys bonefish are generally larger than those used in many other parts of the world. On sparsely vegetated shallows and on deep flats, fast-sinking flies like the Bonefish Special and Clouser Deep Minnow are good choices. When fishing skinny flats with thick turtle grass, slow-sinking and thick-winged flies such as the Frankee-Belle, Snapping Shrimp and Horror not only help eliminate entanglements in dense vegetation, but also land softly on the water and thereby reduce the chances of spooking fish. Patterns that are predominantly brown, tan, yellow, olive or white usually rank as the most productive. I like to match the color of the fly roughly to the bottom of the flat. Hook sizes 2 through 6 work best; size 4 is my favorite overall choice. Use a slow retrieve with 2- to 4-inch strips that hop the fly along the bottom.

For consistent success with Keys bonefish, you'll need to develop good casting technique that allows you to present a fly quickly and accurately even in windy conditions. An angler should be able to accurately cast at least 60 feet with three or fewer false casts. I normally cast 6 or 7 feet in front of and about 2 feet beyond the path of a cruising bonefish. Tailing fish are so intent on feeding that they may only notice a presentation inside of 5 feet.

Depending on wind conditions, fly-fishing outfits between 6- and 9-weight are suitable for big Keys bones. I generally prefer to use a 7-weight during light winds and switch to an 8 as necessary. Reels should hold a minimum of 150 yards of backing, but 200 yards is better. I've had some of my bigger fish get down to the last few turns of backing on the lower-capacity reels.

Floating and intermediate lines will handle any situation a fly-fisher can expect to encounter in the Keys. A floating line sits high on the water making it easier to pick up and recast when a bonefish changes direction — as it often does. It becomes essential in the skinniest flats covered with thick turtle grass, where even the slowest-sinking lines will cause a fly to hang up in the vegetation. On the other hand, a slow-sinking intermediate line gives a fly-fisher better control of both line and fly when windy conditions blow a floating line across the surface. It is especially helpful in getting the fly near the bottom on deep flats. Additionally, the line, leader and fly aren't as likely to collect loose grass and other floating debris when using an intermediate line. Since a delicate presentation is often the key to success, I recommend using 10-pound test tippets with tapered leaders about 10 to 12 feet long.

Wading conditions vary greatly from one area of the Keys to another, and fly-fishers should check the bottom for firm footing before stepping into the water. Throughout most of the Keys the bottom consists mainly of solid sand, but there are portions, particularly on the Florida Bay side, that have a soft mud bottom that makes it almost impossible to wade. Other flats have a hard coral bottom with sharp edges that can prove

hold bonefish. In addition, flats covered with submerged vegetation will contain a variety of crabs, shrimp, sea worms and tiny fish that provide a forage base for bonefish as well as other predators.

As in all types of saltwater angling, an awareness of tidal currents and fluctuations will assist in finding, spotting and casting to bonefish. Shallows directly adjacent to deep water are usually the first places the fish go on an incoming tide. But bonefish may favor different flats during the ebb. Regardless of tidal phase, they typically swim into the current to take advantage of foods and scents that moving water carries to them. Whenever possible, try to station yourself up-current from a bonefish so you can retrieve the fly away from the fish, simulating a frightened prey.

Bonefish are found in the Keys year round, with the best fishing in spring, summer and fall. Bones prefer water temperatures between 72 and 84 degrees, and they will not move up on the flats when the temperature dips below 68 degrees. During extremely hot weather, the fish will usually feed on the flats in the morning and evening when the water is coolest. Extended warm periods in the winter also provide excellent fishing. The best bonefishing I ever experienced in the Keys occurred several years ago in late December before any prolonged cold fronts had a chance to significantly cool the water.

The bonefish has the characteristic mouth of a bottom feeder — upper jaw protruding over the lower — and uses it to root through bottom vegetation, sand, mud and coral in search of food. In extremely shallow water, a bonefish will often go into the classic "tailing" position as it probes. Sometimes rooting bones leave behind little telltale puffs of silt, referred to as "muds." Once prey is captured, a bonefish uses pharyn-

painful to walk on. Thick-soled neoprene flats boots will provide maximum protection from sharp objects and the abrasive effects of sand, shells and other grit.

Once I've located a potentially productive wading flat, I use two methods to find fish. Both involve looking for bones from a typically narrow Keys beach, usually less than 10 feet wide. On long flats with a correspondingly long beach, I like to walk slowly up and down the edge of the beach, looking for signs of bonefish — tails, nervous water or the fish themselves. On smaller flats, I usually bring along a lightweight chair that I place on the highest spot on the beach. From that position I have a good view of any bonefish coming onto the flat. When the fishing is slow, I throw pieces of cut shrimp to chum bonefish into the immediate vicinity. Regardless of the procedure used, a pair of binoculars can be extremely helpful in spotting fish.

Of course, flats skiffs, canoes, kayaks and johnboats give anglers the added mobility to reach more distant spots, and several marinas offer boats for rent. However, a word of caution: Navigating the Keys' waters can be tricky, and boaters should check local charts thoroughly before venturing into unfamiliar areas.

While bonefish rank as the most accessible fish along U.S. 1, permit feed on many of the same flats as well, although they normally frequent deeper water. I sometimes carry a 9- or 10-weight outfit rigged with a Del's Merkin for just such occasions. During late spring and early summer, great numbers of tarpon invade the Keys, but they normally stay on the deeper flats and along banks outside the range of wading fly-fishers. Anglers planning a trip during the peak run will not want to miss the opportunity to catch one of these great fish. You'll need a backcountry skiff to reach the tarpon, but those who don't have a boat and aren't aware of flats etiquette will need the services of a guide. It pays to make a reservation early as the best guides get booked a year or more in advance for the height of the migration. Florida Bay and the nearby Everglades National Park offer excellent fly-fishing for snook and redfish as well.

Unfortunately, there are too many diversions from fishing in the

Florida Keys. Paradise has been paved and developed. A plethora of trendy shops, personal watercraft rentals and tiki bars line much of the Overseas Highway from Key Largo to Key West. Things have changed considerably since I moved away in 1971, when Shorty's diner had a great blue-plate special for a mere pittance and roaming mongrel dogs relieved themselves on the large tree that grew in the center of the Old Anchor Inn, a favorite open-air watering hole. Capt. Tony Terrancino, a local character and former mayor, used to say there were only three things to do in the Keys: fish, drink and (I'll leave the third to the imagination). That truly laid-back lifestyle has given way to today's pervasive pseudo-relaxed atmosphere touted by the Chamber of Commerce. The original flavor of the place has long since disappeared, but a trip on the Overseas Highway remains scenic and can reveal some interesting possibilities, especially when it comes to fly-fishing.

PLANNING A TRIP

You'll find no shortage of things to do in the Keys. The skin and scuba diving on the living coral reefs is outstanding. During lobster season, a quick dive can provide an unbelievably delicious seaside meal when accompanied by lots of drawn butter, fresh corn on the cob and a bottle of your favorite white wine.

The islands have several outstanding parks, including John Pennekamp, Lignum Vitae, Long Key and Bahia Honda. A drive through the Key Deer National Wildlife Refuge may reward you with a rare glimpse of tiny key deer. A trip to historic Key West is also worth the drive.

Rooms are plentiful throughout the Keys. Campers can choose from sites at four state parks or the more stark and expensive commercial campgrounds. You'll need bug repellent if you plan to sleep under the stars. There's no shortage of restaurants either, but don't try to judge menu prices by a restaurant's appearance. Shabbiness is often considered tres chic in the Keys — part of the attempt to appear relaxed and casual, I guess.

SECTION II
THE FISHES

American Shad
Bonefish
Brown Trout
Cubera Snapper
Dolphin
Dorado
Florida Largemouth Bass
Kahawai
Permit
Rainbow Trout
Redfish
Roosterfish
Sailfish
Shark
Snook
Spotted Seatrout
Steelhead
Tarpon
Yellowstone Cutthroat Trout

*Freidrich
Shad Fly*

AMERICAN SHAD
Alosa sapidissima

Family: Clupeidae (Herring)

Other names: Atlantic shad, white shad

Description and identifying characteristics: American shad have metallic-silver flanks with a light-green back and white belly. A large black spot behind the top of the gill cover may be followed by a row of smaller spots. The somewhat rounded mouth of the American shad is what distinguishes it from tarpon.

Size: The average-sized American shad in the St. Johns River weighs around 3 pounds. Larger fish are common but rarely exceed 6 pounds. In the northern part of its range, the fish is somewhat larger.

Life cycle: American shad begin their spawning migration when they reach about 4 to 5 years of age. They spend most of their lives in the cool, deep offshore waters around Canada's Bay of Fundy. Mature fish enter the St. Johns around the first of December to spawn in the river's upper reaches. They lose a tremendous amount of body fat during the long migration. That partially accounts for their 100-percent mortality rate after reproducing, but the comparatively warm water of the St. Johns also saps their energy. (In northern coastal rivers, shad often live to spawn several times, hence, their larger average size.) Newly hatched shad range from 2 to 4 inches long when they leave the river and return to the sea for the cycle to begin again.

Habitat: As anadromous fish, American shad spend most of their lives in salt water, returning to their birth rivers to spawn and subsequently die. In the marine environment, shad prefer deep offshore waters with a temperature between 55 and 65 degrees. During their lives at sea, the fish seasonally move in either a northerly or southerly direction to remain within that preferred temperature range.

Feeding habits: At sea, the shad's diet consists of plankton, but, like many other anadromous fish, they do not feed after entering coastal rivers to spawn.

Horror

BONEFISH
Albula vulpes

Family: Albulidae (Bonefish)

Other names: gray ghost, silver ghost, white fox, ghost-of-the-flats, macabi, *pez raton*

Description and identifying characteristics: Bright silvery sides that reflect the bottom and a barred, light-green back that blends with vegetation make the bonefish difficult to see on the flats. A bonefish uses its protruding upper jaw and long, rounded snout to root along the bottom for food. Powerful pharyngeal teeth, or "crushers," on the isthmus of the tongue, roof of the mouth and throat crush the carapaces and shells of various prey, such as mollusks and crustaceans.

Size: Size varies greatly with geographic location. Bonefish that frequent the flats of the Florida Keys and parts of the Bahamas average between 4 and 6 pounds, with the largest specimens commonly exceeding 10 pounds. With few exceptions, fish in the Yucatán and other parts of the Caribbean are smaller, averaging 2 to 3 pounds. Bones on Pacific flats are comparable to the smaller Caribbean fish. The Seychelle Islands in the Indian Ocean off the southeast coast of Africa have reported catches of fish weighing over 10 pounds. Twenty-pounders have been taken in deep water around Hawaii and southern Africa, but those areas are devoid of suitable flats for the typical shallow-water fly-fishing experience.

Life cycle: Bonefish are generally considered year-around spawners.

Spawning occurs offshore in deep water where newly hatched, ribbon-shaped leptocephalid larvae go through a metamorphosis, shrinking from their original 2 1/2-inch length to develop into tiny juvenile bonefish about an inch long.

Habitat: Bonefish inhabit both deep and shallow waters; however, the fish are most often pursued on the grass, mud, sand, marl and coral flats of the tropics and subtropics. They prefer temperatures between 68 and 86 degrees; fishing is best somewhere between those extremes. Tide and time of day can play an important role in finding productive flats. An incoming tide, with its flood of temperate water, can suddenly warm cold water or cool hot water. Likewise, the middle of a sunny day is a good time to look for bones during chilly weather, while evening and morning prove best in the heat of late summer.

Feeding habits: Several studies have been conducted at different locations to determine the bonefish's food preferences. However, study results vary widely since a bonefish's diet seems to depend more on food availability than on preference. For example, when crustaceans are dominant in an area, they make up a larger part of the bone's diet than mollusks, and vice-versa. Regardless, the bonefish's diet consists almost entirely of crustaceans (crabs and shrimp), mollusks (shellfish), annelids (sea worms) and small fish, depending on accessibility.

BONEFISH GEAR	
FLORIDA KEYS	
Tackle	
Tackle weight	7/8
Rod	8 1/2 to 9'
Line density	F and I
Dacron backing	16 to 20#
Reel capacity	200 yards
Tapered leader	9 to 12'
Tippet	8 to 12#
Flies	
Sand/light grass/ mud/scattered coral—	
Weighted flies	size 1 to 6
Dense grass/thick coral branches—	
Unweighted flies	size 2 to 6
BAHAMAS	
Tackle	
Tackle weight	6/7/8
Rod	8 1/2 to 9'
Line density	F and I
Dacron backing	16 to 20 #
Reel capacity	200 yards
Tapered leader	9 to 12'
Tippet	8 to 12#
Flies	
Sand/light grass/ mud/scattered coral—	
Weighted flies	size 2 to 6
Dense grass/thick coral branches—	
Unweighted flies	size 4 to 6
YUCATÁN	
Tackle	
Tackle weight	5/6/7
Rod	8 1/2 to 9'
Line density	F
Dacron backing	16 to 20#
Reel capacity	150 yards
Tapered leader	9 to 12'
Tippet	6 to 10 #
Flies	
Sand/light grass/ mud/scattered coral—	
Weighted flies	size 4 to 8
Dense grass/thick coral branches—	
Unweighted flies	size 4 to 8

Elk Hair Caddis

BROWN TROUT
Salmo trutta

Family: Salmonidae (trout and salmon)

Other names: German brown trout, brownie, brown

Description and identifying characteristics: Introduced from Europe into the United States in 1883, brown trout are hearty fish. Coloration is a golden brown with shades of olive and bronze. Black spots are scattered about the upper two-thirds of the body, and some specimens also have a few reddish-orange spots along both sides of the lateral line. A light-colored halo surrounds each of the red and black specks.

Size: Average size varies greatly from one body of water to another, but 3/4 to 3-pounders are common in many waters. Fish weighing over 10 pounds are considered significant, but the biggest nonanadromous specimens can exceed 40.

Life cycle: Brown trout spawn in the fall. They are long-lived fish and can survive a dozen or more years, though this is uncommon.

Habitat: Cold-water rivers, streams, tailraces, lakes and impoundments provide prime habitat for brown trout. They can survive in waters from 33 to 75 degrees but prefer temperatures between 54 and 64 degrees. Sensitive to light, browns seek shaded areas such as deep-cut banks, boulders, overhanging bushes and submerged logs during the day.

Feeding habits: Because of their aversion to light, brown trout feed most actively at night, but they will also seek food from shadowy lairs during the day. While their diet is diverse, they can prove highly selective at times. Fish, crustaceans, and terrestrial and aquatic insects make up the major food sources and fly-fishers imitate them most. These fish will sometimes eat amphibians, annelids and tiny mammals as well.

CUBERA SNAPPER
Lutjanus novemfasciatus

Big M Sardine Fly

Family: Lutjanidae (snapper)

Other names: dog snapper, black snapper, *pargo negro*

Description and identifying characteristics: Four prominent canine teeth have given rise to one of the Pacific cubera's nicknames: dog snapper. Adult fish are dark red with vertical bars along the flanks.

Size: Only slightly smaller than its Atlantic cousin, the Pacific cubera grows to around 80 pounds.

Life cycle: Spawning is believed to occur in late summer.

Habitat: The cubera frequents rocks, reefs, ledges and underwater caves from inshore shallows to depths of approximately 100 feet. They sometimes congregate in schools of 100 or more fish. These same waters will often hold mullet snapper (*L. aratus*) as well. This snapper — easily distinguished from other snappers by its rounded snout and mullet-shaped head — grow to 40 pounds, though anything over 20 is considered a trophy.

Feeding habits: Pacific cubera are voracious feeders, especially at night. Prey includes finfish, some of which are surprisingly large, and crustaceans, including large lobsters.

SNAPPER GEAR

PACIFIC CUBERA SNAPPER

Tackle

Tackle weight	10 to 13
Rod	8 1/2 to 9'
Line density	SH-F and S Type IV
Running line	30 to 35# flat mono
Dacron backing	30#
Reel capacity	200 to 250 yards
Tippet	20#
Wire shock	40# braided micro wire

Flies

Large Streamer	size 1/0 to 3/0
Hair Bug	size 1/0 to 3/0
Foam Popper	size 1/0 to 3/0

MULLET SNAPPER

Tackle

Tackle weight	10 to 12
Rod	8 1/2 to 9'
Line density	SH-F and S Type IV
Running line	30 to 35# flat mono
Dacron backing	30#
Reel capacity	200 to 250 yards
Tippet	20#
Wire shock	40# braided micro wire

Flies

Large Streamer	size 1/0 to 3/0
Hair Bug	size 1/0 to 3/0
Foam Popper	size 1/0 to 3/0

Lefty's Deceiver

DOLPHIN
Coryphaena hippurus

Family: Coryphaenidae (Dolphin)

Other names: dorado, mahimahi, dolphinfish

Description and identifying characteristics: One of the most colorful of all fish, dolphin have an iridescent bluish-green back and dorsal fin with a golden underbelly and tail. Male "bull" dolphin have flat foreheads that distinguish them from the round-headed juveniles and female "cows." Dolphin show strong schooling instincts and tend to congregate according to age. Once hooked, they become acrobatic leapers.

Size: The dolphin grows phenomenally fast, reaching a weight of about 13 pounds by the end of the first year and as much as 80 pounds by the fourth.

Life cycle: Dolphin are prolific breeders that spawn between April and August, depending on latitude. Young fish often gather around concentrations of floating Sargassum weed, where they become part of an intricate food web that includes a variety of marine life. Life expectancy is short — only five years.

Habitat: Dolphin inhabit warm, deep, temperate seas and ocean currents such as the Gulf Stream. Nevertheless, they sometimes venture closer to shore. From birth, the fish have a strong attachment to floating Sargassum, as well as other flotsam and jetsam. Current rips are another favorite hang out. As the fish grow larger they tend to roam the open sea as pelagics. They prefer water temperatures of 68 degrees or higher.

Feeding habits: As large predators near the top of the marine food chain, adult dolphin feed on a variety of fishes and cephalopods, including flying fish, mackerel, ballyhoo, squid and even smaller juvenile dolphin. Their incredible speed makes them highly efficient hunters.

DORADO
Salminus maxillosus

Blanton's Whistler

Family: Characidae (Dorado)

Other names: tiger of the water

Description and identifying characteristics: The dorado's Spanish name is derived from its brilliant golden color. At first glance, they have the appearance of some fictitious exotic salmon species, but they are not related to any of the salmonids. Like the salmonids, however, dorado are tough opponents on the fly rod and one of the strongest fish in fresh water. They are also great leapers. Dorado have a formidable double row of teeth with prominent canines that demand the attention of any fly-fisher lucky enough to catch one. Four species comprise the Salminus genus, all located in major river systems of South America, but *S. maxillosus* is the largest.

Size: Dorado average slightly under 5 pounds on the Paraná River with the largest ones, *"dorado grande,"* reaching as much as 75 pounds or more.

Life cycle: The dorado's mating ritual is much like that of salmon. Between January and March, dorado follow a migratory route upstream toward the Paraná's headwaters, where the fish will spawn in the shade of one of the river's tributaries. While a female digs out a redd with her tail, males fight for the right to mate with her.

Habitat: Large rocks and other submerged debris shelter dorado from swift river currents and provide prime ambush spots from which to attack prey.

Feeding habits: Much of the dorado's life is controlled by the availability of *sabalo* (a freshwater baitfish not to be confused with tarpon), the primary forage base of dorado. Dorado follow the small fish as they move in schools up and down the river.

DORADO GEAR

SCHOOL DORADO
Tackle

Tackle weight	7/8
Line density	SH F to Type IV S
Rod	8 1/2 to 9'
Dacron backing	20#
Running line	braided/flat mono, fly line
Reel capacity	150 yards
Leader	tapered or big-game
Tippet	10 to 16#
Wire Shock	26# braided micro wire

Flies

Wobbler	size 2 to 2/0
Blanton's Whistler	size 1/0 to 3/0
Clouser Minnow	size 1 to 2/0

DORADO GRANDE
Tackle

Tackle weight	8/9
Line density	SH F to Type IV S
Rod	8 1/2 to 9'
Dacron backing	20#
Running line	braided/flat mono, fly line
Reel capacity	150 yards
Leader	tapered or big-game
Tippet	16 to 20#
Wire Shock	26# braided micro wire

Flies

Wobbler	size 1/0 to 2/0
Blanton's Whistler	size 1/0 to 3/0
Clouser Minnow	size 1 to 2/0

FLORIDA LARGEMOUTH BASS

Micropterus salmoides floridanus

BASS GEAR

OPEN WATER/ LIGHT VEGETATION

Tackle

Tackle weight	6/7/8
Line density	F and F/S Type III
Rod	8 1/2 to 9'
Dacron backing	20#
Reel capacity	100 yards
Tapered leader	7 1/2 to 10'(F); 5 to 7 1/2' (F/S)
Tippet	12 to 16#

Flies

Popper	size 4 to 1/0
Clouser Minnow	size 4 to 1/0
Eelworm Streamer	size 2 to 1/0
Misc. streamers	size 2 to 1/0

HEAVY VEGETATION

Tackle

Tackle weight	7/8
Line density	F
Rod	8 1/2 to 9'
Dacron backing	20#
Reel capacity	100 yards
Tapered leader	7 1/2 to 10'
Tippet	12 to 16#

Flies

Popper	size 4 to 1/0
Eelworm Streamer	size 2 to 1/0
Misc. streamers	size 2 to 1/0

Family: Centrarchidae (Sunfish)

Other names: black bass, green trout (early name), big-mouth bass

Description and identifying characteristics: The Florida largemouth is a subspecies of the largemouth bass. The main distinguishing characteristics of the Florida version is the scale counts at different body locations and, more important, its larger size. Its coloration can vary from a dark brownish-green in dark waters to a more metallic green in clearer water. The jaw hinge of all largemouth bass extends past the eye when the mouth closes; that differentiates them from all other bass species. Although the Florida subspecies is native only to Florida, it has been introduced into other areas with great success. The fish commonly breed with their northern cousins in Georgia. Once considered a regional inhabitant of still, eutrophic waters, the primary species of largemouth, *M. salmoides*, has been introduced into waters all over the world, including Mexico, Canada and the entire United States.

Size: Ten-pound fish are caught with regularity throughout the state, and on rare occasions a few may reach 20 pounds. Average size is 2 to 4 pounds. Females grow larger than males.

Life cycle: Spawning usually begins in early spring when the water temperature reaches 67 degrees. In addition to fertilizing the female's eggs, males play a significant role in the spawning process by building the nest, guarding it during incubation and protecting the fry for several days after the eggs hatch. Juveniles grow rapidly and reach sexual maturity by their second year. Bass may live as long as 13 years.

Habitat: Florida largemouth inhabit the brackish waters of upper estuaries as well as freshwater streams, lakes, ponds and impoundments. These bass only occasionally venture outside the aquatic plant zone or away from submerged structure.

Feeding habits: The Florida largemouth's diet includes frogs, gizzard shad, crayfish, insects, threadfin shad, shiners and other sunfish.

KAHAWAI
Arripis trutta

Clouser Deep Minnow

Family: Arripidae

Other names: Australian salmon

Description and identifying characteristics: Although they are not related to any of the salmonids, kahawai have a salmonlike appearance, hence, their nickname. They have a bluish-green back and sides with gray, bronze and gold spots that graduate into a silvery belly. *A. esper*, another species of kahawai and a close relative of *A. trutta*, ranges along Australia's western shore.

Size: Although in some rare instances kahawai may top 16 pounds, the average fish probably weighs about 4 to 5 pounds.

Life cycle: The spawning season in New Zealand waters occurs between November and February. Kahawai reach sexual maturity in the fourth or fifth year.

Habitat: Kahawai are pelagic fishes that roam the rocky coastal waters of Tasmania, eastern Australia and New Zealand. Large schools often congregate in estuaries and bays where their surface feeding often attracts a large number of seabirds. Sometimes the schools are less conspicuous: Occasional surface boils and swirls are the only indications that kahawai are in an area. Their migratory patterns depend largely on the availability of zooplankton and pods of baitfish.

Feeding habits: The kahawai's diet is composed almost entirely of zooplankton, especially tiny shrimp, and small fish such as herring and anchovies. In heavy concentrations of zooplankton, kahawai will sometimes swim with their mouths open to ingest as much of the krill as possible.

KAHAWAI GEAR

Tackle

Tackle weight	8/9/10
Line density	SH Type IV S
Rod	8 1/2 to 9'
Dacron backing	20#
Reel capacity	200 yards
Tapered leader	6 to 7 1/2'
Tippet	8 to 16#
Optional Shock	30#

Flies

Clouser Minnow	size 1 to 2/0
Lefty's Deceiver	size 1 to 2/0

Del's Merkin

PERMIT
Trachinotus falcatus

Family: Carangidae (jack and pompano)

Other names: great pompano, palometa

Description and identifying characteristics: Permit have a bluish-gray back that fades into bright silver sides. These reflect the bottom coloration and camouflage the fish in any kind of habitat. The belly has a brilliant orange-yellow patch between the anal and pelvic fins. The permit's deep body is more angular at the dorsal and anal fins than the elongated and curved body of pompano (*T. carolinus*), a smaller close relative. When tailing on the flats, the permit's dark, almost black fins are easily differentiated from those of the silvery bonefish.

Size: Fish between 5 and 20 pounds are common, with occasional specimens topping 50 pounds. Permit in the Caribbean generally run smaller than those in the Bahamas and the Florida Keys, where the biggest fish are consistently taken.

Life cycle: Despite its popularity, relatively little is known about the permit's life cycle. Most believe that spawning occurs offshore. After hatching, the young slowly migrate toward shore to mature. Small permit tend to congregate in schools, becoming more solitary with age.

Habitat: Permit and bonefish frequent many of the same flats, but permit, because of their larger size, prefer deeper water. Permit especially like flats that lie directly adjacent to channels and drop-offs.

Feeding habits: The bulk of the permit's diet consists of crustaceans, mollusks, sea urchins and small fish. Crabs are a favorite prey and the one that successful fly-fishers most often imitate.

Olive Parachute

RAINBOW TROUT
Oncorhynchus mykiss

Family: Salmonidae (trout)

Other names: 'bow

Description and identifying characteristics: Rainbow trout are native to North America's West Coast, though they have been introduced into many waters worldwide. As with most fish species, habitat plays a big role in the fish's coloration. In general, the dorsal region is green and graduates to a bluish tone, then to silver. A broad strip of pink or red follows the lateral line from just behind the eye to the tail. Small black spots spread over the upper portion of the body.

Size: Size varies significantly at different locales. Nonanadromous rainbows may grow larger than 50 pounds, but fish under 4 pounds are the norm in most waters.

Life cycle: For nonanadromous rainbows, the spawning season occurs from January through June, but it can occur as late as August at high elevations. Life expectancy is seven to 11 years.

Habitat: Rainbows flourish in cold-water rivers, streams, tailraces, lakes and reservoirs. They tolerate warm environments better than browns: They can survive in water over 80 degrees, but prefer temperatures below 70 degrees.

Feeding habits: Aquatic and terrestrial insects, small fish, crayfish and freshwater shrimp make up the most important food sources for rainbows. On occasion, they may also feed on small mice, worms, frogs and salamanders. When the fish become selective eaters, a fly-fisher must "match the hatch."

RAINBOW GEAR	
Tackle	
Tackle weight	4/5/6
Line density	F and F/S Type III
Rod	8 1/2 to 10'
Dacron backing	16 to 20 #
Reel capacity	100 yards
Tapered leader	9 to 14'
Dry fly tippet	4X to 7X
Nymph tippet	2X to 4X
Streamer tippet	0X to 1X
Flies	
Caddis	Nymphs
Mayflies	Emergers
Stoneflies	Spinners
Hoppers	Attractor Dries
Streamers	

Cave's Wobbler

REDFISH
Sciaenops ocellata

Family: Sciaenidae (drum)

Other names: channel bass, red drum, red, puppy drum (juvenile)

Description and identifying characteristics: Redfish have a bronze tone that deepens in color when the fish swims over dark sea-grass beds and become increasingly subdued against a light, sand bottom. Tannin-stained waters give them a yellowish hue. The fish use a snub nose and inferior mouth to probe the bottom for food. Adults have a black spot on the upper sides at the base of the tail. Juvenile fish often have several spots throughout their length; most disappear with maturity.

Size: Big fish are called "bull reds" even though they are usually females. The largest recorded red weighed 90 pounds, but anything over 35 pounds is considered an exceptional fish. Average size varies greatly from one geographic location to another, with 6- to 10-pounders common in most areas.

Life cycle: Males reach sexual maturity between their first and third years, while females develop between 3 to 6 years of age. Spawning occurs in late summer, fall and even early winter when water tempera- tures hover around 71 to 86 degrees. Reds spawn at night along ocean beaches, passes, inlets and estuaries with high salinity. Currents trans- port the larvae into estuaries, where they develop into juvenile redfish and remain until their third or fourth year. In some regions, some fish leave the estuaries for the sea, while in other areas they stay in estuaries or move to nearby bays. Redfish grow rapidly, about 15 inches in the first year, and are long-lived, reaching more than 50 years old.

Habitat: Redfish are euryhaline, or tolerant of widely varied salinity levels, and easily survive in fresh and salt waters. Habitat ranges from freshwater rivers and inshore flats to offshore waters. Fly-fishers gener- ally target these fish in estuaries and bays where they congregate around grass and mud flats, oyster bars, drop-offs, sand bars, potholes and slight depressions or shallow channels.

Feeding habits: Availability of prey ranks as the biggest influence on the redfish's diet. On the flats, the bulk of the forage base usually consists of crustaceans, especially crabs and shrimp, but small horseshoe crabs, worms and finfish are all part of the redfish's diet.

ROOSTERFISH
Nematistius pectoralis

Sea Habit Deceiver

Family: Nematisiidae (roosterfish)

Other names: rooster, *papagallo, pez gallo*

Description and identifying characteristics: Roosterfish derive their name from the elongated spines on the first dorsal fin. Most say the dorsal resembles a cock's comb, while others maintain that it looks like the hackles on a rooster's tail. Regardless of the origin, roosters are exquisitely beautiful. These fish are predominantly white with bluish-black stripes that curve down from the trademark dorsal fin toward the caudal fin. The dorsal has bluish-black stripes as well.

Size: Roosters can grow to over 100 pounds, but the average falls closer to the 10- to 25-pound range. Small roosters gather in schools of less than a dozen similarly sized fish, but the bigger ones are more solitary.

Life cycle: Little is known about the life history of roosterfish, but they probably don't wander over a wide range — not more than 300 miles.

Habitat: Roosterfish occur in large numbers only in the central portion of the Pacific, from Baja California to Peru. There they inhabit nearshore waters and prefer rocky outcroppings around the surf zone. Sometimes they move along sandy beaches only a few feet from shore.

Feeding habits: Tides play a major role in roosterfish movement and feeding habits. The fish will suddenly become active at the onset of an incoming tide and turn off just as quickly when the tide turns. Their diet consists almost entirely of small finfish. When feeding or otherwise stimulated, the rooster raises its famous dorsal fin — an exciting scene when it protrudes above the water surface.

ROOSTERFISH GEAR

Tackle

Tackle weight	9/10/11
Rod	8 1/2 to 9'
Line density	SH F to IV S
Running line	30 to 35# flat mono
Dacron backing	30#
Reel capacity	200 to 250 yards
Tippet	12 to 20#
Shock	50#

Flies

Lefty's Deceiver	size 2/0 to 3/0
Popper	size 1/0 to 3/0
Misc. 8" streamers	size 2/0 to 3/0

SAILFISH
Istiophorus platypterus

ATLANTIC SAILFISH
Tackle

Tackle weight	12 to 15
Rod	8 to 9'
Line density	SH Type IV S
Running line	30 to 35# flat mono
Dacron backing	30#
Reel capacity	250 yards plus
Tippet	12 to 20#
Shock	100#

Flies

Tandem-hook poppers	size 3/0 to 5/0
Tandem-hook streamers	size 3/0 to 5/0

PACIFIC SAILFISH
Tackle

Tackle weight	12 to 15
Rod	8 to 9'
Line density	SH Type IV S
Running line	30 to 35# flat mono
Dacron backing	30#
Reel capacity	250 yards plus
Tippet	12 to 20#
Shock	100#

Flies

Tandem-hook poppers	size 4/0 to 5/0
Tandem-hook streamers	size 4/0 to 5/0

Family: Istiophoridae (billfish)

Other names: sail, *pez vela*

Description and identifying characteristics: The large, saillike dorsal fin marks the sailfish's most dominant feature and the reason for its name. Like all Istiophoid fish, it has another dominant feature, an elongated bill that some say aids in its feeding. The dorsal fin is cobalt blue with numerous small black spots; the cobalt back fades into brownish-blue and then to a silvery underside. Fifteen or more vertical lines of light-blue spots occur evenly along the sides. Long, slender pelvic fins extend almost to the anal fin. Taxonomically, many consider Atlantic and Pacific sailfish the same species, though some experts believe otherwise. While less is known about Pacific sailfish than those in the Atlantic, their diet, habitat and life history closely parallel that of Atlantic fish. The major difference is size.

Size: The largest Pacific fish can surpass 200 pounds in weight, while the largest Atlantic specimens reach roughly half that size. Size in the Atlantic fluctuates with location, but the most commonly encountered size ranges between 40 and 45 pounds with a length of roughly 7 feet. A fish topping 100 pounds is considered a real trophy throughout the world's oceans.

Life cycle: Courtship for Atlantic sails usually begins inshore between mid-May and September, when one to three males compete for the attention of a ripe female on the water's surface. They grow rapidly to 4 to 5 feet in length and roughly 20 pounds in the first year. Life expectancy is at least seven years and may be as long as 10.

Habitat: Sailfish prefer tropical and subtropical oceanic waters where the temperature remains between 77 and 82 degrees and water depth exceeds 6 fathoms. Migratory patterns tend to follow food sources and seasonal temperature variations. In the Northern Hemisphere, that means a northerly migration as the water heats up and a southerly movement when it cools.

Feeding habits: Jacks, herrings, ballyhoo, mackerel, flying fish, sardines, mullet, tuna, needlefish, squid and octopus make up the mainstays of the sailfish's diet; however, sails eat any number of other small fish species. During peak migratory periods when large schools of baitfish are present, several sailfish will swim with dorsal fins extended around the bait in ever-tightening circles in a procedure known as "balling the bait." Once the small fish pack tightly together, the sailfish move in for the kill.

SHARK
Chondrichthyes

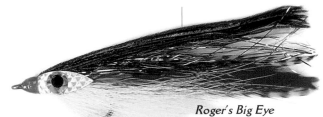

Roger's Big Eye Baitfish

Class: Chondrichthyes (cartilaginous fishes)

Description and identifying characteristics: In contrast to other fishes which have a bony skeleton, sharks have a skeleton made of cartilage that allows them great flexibility. They have two rows of teeth that periodically fall out and are replaced by new ones. Shark skin is roughly textured with tiny, toothlike points called "denticles." In most species, the upper half of the tail, or caudal fin, is larger than the lower half.

Size: Size varies widely from one species to another, from 2 to 60 feet. Scientists consider 6 feet to be the average length of all combined shark members. Size, however, does not indicate temperament or aggressive-ness. The largest of sharks, the whale shark, is a gentle, somewhat lethargic giant that feeds on plankton, squid and small schooling fishes.

Life cycle: Most species bear live young, although a few lay eggs. The largest sharks may prove especially long-lived.

Habitat: Sharks are found throughout the seas of the world. Numerous species inhabit shallow flats, while many prefer a reef environment and still others favor the open sea.

Feeding habits: Sharks primarily eat meat, but studies of the stomach contents of different species have revealed that in most instances they feed opportunistically and will eat just about anything.

SHARK GEAR

SHALLOW FLATS:
(SMALL SHARK)
Tackle

Tackle weight	7/8
Rod	8 1/2 to 9'
Line density	F and I
Running line	NA
Dacron backing	20#
Reel capacity	200 yards
Tippet	12 to 16#
Wire shock	.014 single-strand

Flies

Misc. streamers	size 1 to 1/0

MODERATE DEPTH:
(MEDIUM SHARK)
Tackle

Tackle weight	9/10
Rod	8 1/2 to 9'
Line density	SH Type IV
Running line	30 to 35# flat mono
Dacron backing	20 to 30#
Reel capacity	200 to 250 yards
Tippet	16 to 20#
Wire shock	.014 single-strand

Flies

Misc. streamers	size 1/0 to 3/0

OPEN SEA:
(LARGE SHARK)
Tackle

Tackle weight	12/15
Rod	8 to 9'
Line density	SH Type IV
Running line	30 to 35# flat mono
Dacron backing	30#
Reel capacity	250 yards
Tippet	20#
Wire shock	.016 single-strand

Flies

Misc. streamers	size 3/0 to 5/0

<table>
</table>

Finger Mullet Hair Bug

SNOOK
Centropomus unidecimalis

Family: Centropomidae (snook)

Other names: saltwater pike, snuke, linesider, sergeant fish, *robalo*

Description and identifying characteristics: The common snook's most distinguishing characteristic is a long, black lateral line that runs from the top of the operculum (gill cover) to the back of the caudal fin. The head is slightly concave on top, and the lower jaw protrudes beyond the upper maxillary. Habitat plays an important role in coloration, which can vary from golden brown to dark bronze with silvery-white flanks and stomach.

Size: Maximum weight runs to approximately 50 pounds, with the average fish around 5 to 8 pounds. Most anglers rank anything over 25 pounds a highly prized catch.

Life cycle: Spawning takes place around river mouths, inlets and passes between April and November, but peak season runs from June through July. Studies indicate that snook may have a life span of about 20 years.

Habitat: Common snook are found within the tropics and the subtropics. They prefer various nearshore habitats, including bays, rivers, inlets, estuaries and, occasionally, bodies of freshwater where they tend to hang around sunken trees, deep-cut banks, docks, current edges, bars and overhanging shrubs. In Florida, mangrove-lined waters mark the preeminent environments. Sensitive to cold, snook can't tolerate water temperatures much below 60 degrees. Consequently, winter cold snaps often result in significant fish kills, especially in the northernmost extremes in the snook's range. They prefer water between 80 to 85 degrees, but can live satisfactorily in water as hot as 90 degrees.

Feeding habits: Snook feed mainly on fish, but crustaceans — especially crabs and shrimp — also rank as a significant part of their diet. Snook like to hide in cover, from which they can attack unsuspecting prey. Mangrove edges offer primary ambush spots during a falling tide, when bait and crustaceans emerge from the protective root system.

SPOTTED SEATROUT

Cynoscion nebulosus

Family: Sciaenidae (drum)

Other names: trout, gator trout (large specimens), spotted weakfish, speckled trout, speck

Description and identifying characteristics: Spotted seatrout are an iridescent bluish-green and gray with a silver belly and small black spots along the upper half of the body. The lower jaw protrudes beyond the upper jaw, which has two large teeth at the tip.

Size: Maximum size appears to be just under 20 pounds, with the average fish weighing 2 to 3 pounds. In Florida, big seatrout are frequently referred to as "gator trout."

Life cycle: The spawning season takes place between March and November in deeper portions of estuaries. The small larva and fry develop in areas with thick marine vegetation. Spotted seatrout show strong schooling tendencies until about the fourth or fifth year, after which they become increasingly solitary. The typical lifespan appears to be at least 10 years.

Habitat: Because they can tolerate widely varied salinity levels, spotted seatrout are ideally adapted to living in estuaries. Lush, grassy shallows are almost synonymous with the fish, but oyster beds, creek mouths, submerged structure and drop-offs also hold fish. Spotted seatrout are temperature-sensitive and prefer water between 59 and 86 degrees. During winter cold snaps, the trout seek refuge in deep holes. Severe temperature drops in the winter can kill fish stranded in shallow water.

Feeding habits: Penaeid shrimp (white, pink and brown) and small finfish make up the mainstays in the spotted seatrout's diet. As trout grow, finfish become increasingly important as a food source. However, the fish's eating habits are based more on food availability than on a preference of one prey over another.

SEATROUT GEAR

SHALLOW FLATS

Tackle

Tackle weight	6/7/8
Line density	F
Rod	8 1/2 to 9'
Dacron backing	20#
Reel capacity	150 yards
Tapered leader	9 to 10'
Tippet	10 to 16#

Flies

Rattlin' Minnow	size 1/0
Popper	size 1 to 2/0
Bendback	size 1 to 1/0
Clouser Minnow	size 2 to 2/0
Wobbler	size 2 to 2/0

DEEP FLATS

Tackle

Tackle weight	6/7/8
Line density	F, I, F/S Type III
Rod	8 1/2 to 9'
Dacron backing	20#
Reel capacity	150 yards
Tapered leader	9 to 10'
Tippet	10 to 16#

Flies

Rattlin' Minnow	size 1/0
Popper	size 1 to 2/0
Bendback	size 1 to 1/0
Clouser Minnow	size 2 to 2/0
Wobbler	size 2 to 2/0

DEEP HOLES

Tackle

Tackle weight	7/8
Line density	F/S 250 grain
Rod	8 1/2 to 9'
Dacron backing	20#
Reel capacity	150 yards
Tapered leader	9 to 10'
Tippet	10 to 16 #

Flies

Lefty's Deceiver	size 1 to 2/0
Clouser Minnow	size 2 to 2/0
Wobbler	size 2 to 2/0

STEELHEAD
Oncorhynchus mykiss

Purple Peril

Family: Salmonidae (trout and salmon)

Other names: steelie, sea-run rainbow

Description and identifying characteristics: Steelhead are sea-run rainbow trout. Fresh from the sea, the fish have a silvery steel-gray color that darkens and takes on a rainbowlike appearance as the journey continues upriver.

Size: A steelhead's size depends greatly on the number of years it spends feeding on marine life before returning to fresh water. Four-year-old first-time spawners are bigger than those three years of age, and so on. In their fourth year, steelhead may weigh 20 to 35 pounds. The largest fish top 40 pounds.

Life cycle: As anadromous fish, they migrate from their marine environment to spawn in the freshwater rivers and streams of their origin. This ritual takes place sometime between the steelhead's first and fourth year at sea. Depending on the strain of steelhead and its birth water, about 5 to 15 percent of spawning fish live to reproduce again. They may live as long as seven years in rare instances.

Habitat: Steelhead spend the largest portion of their lives in a marine environment. During their spawning run, they usually travel in the first 3 feet of the water column, stopping to rest around holes and underwater obstructions, but they avoid placid and exceedingly shallow water.

Feeding habits: Steelhead generally do not eat during their freshwater spawning run. Any feeding response probably occurs as the result of instinctive behavior rather than hunger.

TARPON
Megalops atlanticus

Red/Black Tarpon

Family: Elopidae (tarpon)

Other names: silver king, 'poon, *sabalo*

Description and identifying characteristics: Tarpon have a blue or green back that varies from a light metallic appearance to very dark. The rest of the fish is silvery except in tannin-colored water where the flanks take on a golden tone. The large, bony mouth has a protruding lower jaw that turns upward. They resemble fictional giant herring. Tarpon are great leapers when hooked.

Size: Regardless of whether you seek giant fish that top 100 pounds or babies weighing just a few pounds, tarpon are considered one of saltwater fly-fishing's top prizes. The largest specimens can exceed 280 pounds.

Life cycle: Tarpon gather in coastal areas during late spring and early summer just before they migrate to offshore spawning areas. Throughout much of the tarpon's range, the spawning season runs between May and September. They breed prolifically, and a large, ripe female can disperse as many as 12 million eggs. Newly hatched leptocephalid larvae metamorphose into tiny juveniles. They grow rather slowly and, based on new scientific aging techniques, may live at least 55 years.

Habitat: Tarpon inhabit both fresh and salt waters. They can survive in stagnant water by using a lunglike air bladder to take in oxygen from the atmosphere when they roll on the surface. Baby and small tarpon live in brackish estuaries, canals, tidal creeks and bodies of fresh water that lie close to the coast. Larger fish mainly inhabit open waters, coastal rivers, inlets, deep flats and passes. Primarily warm-water fish, tarpon become stressed when temperatures dip below 55 degrees.

Feeding habits: Fish and crustaceans, especially crabs, make up the bulk of the tarpon's diet. In the Florida Keys, the fish will feed rather selectively during the palolo worm hatch that usually takes place in May.

TARPON GEAR

FLORIDA
Tackle

Tackle Weight	10 - 13
Rod	8 1/2 - 9'
Line Density	I, mono F/S
Dacron Backing	30#
Reel Capacity	250 yards
Tippet	12-20#
Shock	80-100#

Flies

Keys Style	3/0 - 4/0
Bunny Style	3/0 - 4/0

CENTRAL AMERICA
Tackle

Tackle Weight	11 - 13
Rod	8 1/2 - 9'
Line Density	I, SH Type IV
Running Line	30-35#
Dacron Backing	30#
Reel Capacity	250 yards
Tippet	16-20#
Shock	80-100#

Flies

Blanton's Whistler	3/0 - 5/0

YUCATÁN
Tackle

Tackle Weight	9 - 11
Rod	8 1/2 - 9'
Line Density	I, mono F/S
Dacron Backing	30#
Reel Capacity	225 yards
Tippet	12-20#
Shock	80-100#

Flies

Keys Style	3/0
Bunny Style	3/0

BABY TARPON
Tackle

Tackle Weight	4 - 9
Rod	8 - 9'
Line Density	F and I
Dacron Backing	16-20#
Reel Capacity	150 yards
Tippet	6-16#
Shock	20-60#

Flies

Keys Style	4 - 1/0
Bunny Style	4 - 1/0
Small Streamers	4 - 1/0
Popper	2 - 1/0

Dave's Hopper

CUTTHROAT GEAR

Tackle

Tackle weight	4/5/6
Line density	F
Rod	8 ¹/₂ to 10'
Dacron backing	16 to 20#
Reel capacity	100 yards
Tapered leader	9 to 12'
Dry fly tippet	4X to 7X
Nymph tippet	2X to 4X
Streamer tippet	0X to 1X

Flies

Caddis	Nymphs
Mayflies	Emergers
Stoneflies	Spinners
Hoppers	Attractor Dries
Streamers	

YELLOWSTONE CUTTHROAT

Oncorhynchus clarki bouvieri

Family: Salmonidae (trout and salmon)

Other names: cut, native trout

Description and identifying characteristics: There are many sub-species of cutthroat trout, each with widely different coloration. The Yellowstone strain is typically caramel-colored with red gill covers and the trademark red slashes on the throat. The fish has dark spots over its entire length, but they are especially numerous toward the posterior.

Size: Two- to 3-pound cutthroat are common in many of Yellowstone's rivers, streams and lakes, and bigger ones are not at all unusual. The largest cutthroat (all subspecies included) ever recorded was a 41-pound Lahontan taken in 1925, a strain that averaged about 20 pounds but is, unfortunately, now almost extinct. Only populations maintained through stocking programs remain.

Life cycle: Adults spawn every other year, usually between late spring and early summer. Many believe that cuts may live for about 12 years.

Habitat: Yellowstone cuts inhabit many of the lakes, rivers and streams within Yellowstone National Park. Populations are highly susceptible to fishing pressure. Furthermore, their tendency to hybridize, especially with rainbows, has led to the depletion of pure stock.

Feeding habits: Cutthroat feed primarily on fish, crustaceans, and terrestrial and aquatic insects. Like other species of trout, they can prove selective, focusing on only one food source.

THE GEAR
Advice for the Traveling Fly-Fisher

During the lifetime that I've been involved in fly-fishing, I've managed to acquire vast collections of rods, reels, fly lines and the other miscellaneous equipment that we use on the water. In that time, I've learned that quality is indeed remembered long after price is forgotten. That said, I've also seen plenty of examples of price not necessarily equating to quality. The problem is, you don't want to be on a flat thousands of miles from home when you discover the difference. The information contained below will be old hat to some, and insightful to others. It is intended to help anglers learn more about how to evaluate their tackle, especially in light of the high demands that traveling can place on fly gear.

Rods

Almost all airlines require that two-piece rods be checked through as baggage; consequently, I would discourage anyone from traveling with two-piece fly rods. My experience has been they're all too often lost in transit. In almost all cases, three-, four- and five-piece travel rods qualify as carry-on luggage and are easily placed in the overhead storage bins of most large jets. They also fit easily into the luggage compartments of small planes. More important, anglers sacrifice nothing in the way of performance when using well-designed multisection rods. Although some of the best can cost more than $500, many excellent inexpensive models also exist.

All good rods have several features in common, regardless of price or manufacturer. They must dampen quickly, have quality components, be lightweight, feature an excellent warranty and have an action that will improve the fly-fisher's casting skills.

Dampening refers to a rod's ability to stop vibrating after the stop at the end of the stroke on both the forward and backcasts. A rod that continues to vibrate after the stop will create waves in the fly line instead of a smooth loop. To test a rod's dampening characteristic, hold the rod parallel to the floor with a relaxed grip on the cork handle. Shake the tip firmly, but not harshly, a few inches toward the floor so that the rod oscillates up and down. Heavy rods need to be shaken harder than those designed to cast light lines. Then, using the finger tips and thumb on the opposite hand, quickly grab the rod about 16 inches above the cork grip and immediately release it. A quality rod will stop oscillating almost instantly. Years ago, the worst rods would continue to vibrate as if they were in perpetual motion like the pendulum on a clock. However, differences in most of today's rods are usually subtle.

Premier carbon-fiber fly rods feature the highest-quality lightweight graphite and come fitted with AA cork grips, reel seats machined to tight tolerances, titanium or chrome-plated snake guides and one or more high-quality stripping guides. On the other hand, less expensive blanks, species cork (with more imperfections), graphite reels seats, stainless

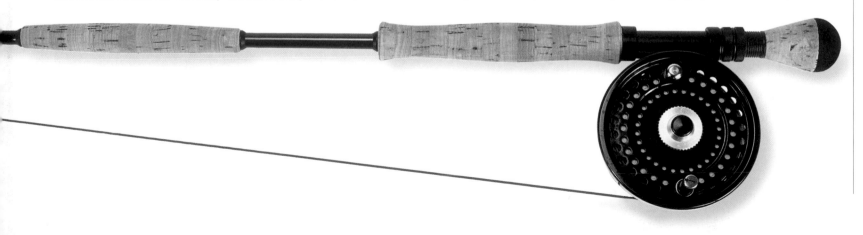

snake guides and ceramic stripping guide(s) are economical components used on some less costly models. Still, these are not necessarily indications of a "bad" rod, only an inexpensive one. Regardless of price, good rods will have at least one guide per foot of rod; a 9-foot rod will have nine or more guides, including seven or eight snake guides and one or two stripping guides, plus the tip-top. Comparatively small guides, sloppy metal reel seats and foam grips generally indicate poor quality.

The durability of graphite rods has improved considerably since their introduction in the early 1970s. Nevertheless, breakage can still prove problematic whether a rod snaps while fighting a big fish or breaks in a car door. Several manufacturers offer amazingly long warranties, some extending over a lifetime, regardless of how the rod breaks. That can be the major factor in deciding which rod to buy.

Rod action remains a rather controversial subject because everyone seems to have an opinion about which action is best: slow, medium, fast or progressive. "Action" refers to the way a rod bends when loaded with either the weight of a fish or a fly line. A "slow" rod flexes parabolically throughout its length regardless of the load. A rod with "medium" action bends primarily through the upper half of its length, while a "fast" rod will load primarily toward the tip. A "progressive-action" rod flexes progressively down the blank as the load increases or as more line is false cast. Some anglers like the deliberateness of slow action when making short casts to small fish on a narrow stream. For others, the strong butt section of a fast rod can be an advantage when fighting large fish. While I generally prefer the excellent all-around casting and fish-fighting qualities of a progressive rod, there is no one best action. Each angler must decide for himself which rod provides the most overall pleasure under a specific set of circumstances. Try out several different actions to find the one that's best for you.

Reels

Not that long ago, only a few manufacturers produced exquisitely machined reels with satin-smooth drags. Now there are too many to mention, much to the angler's advantage. For the fastest and most powerful fish, I like the benefits large-arbor models offer. But standard spools remain popular, too, and I still use them in some freshwater and saltwater applications, especially for smaller fish such as bass, trout, reds and bonefish.

When travelling, I usually take along a variety of reels; however, where weight is a factor, Charlton configurable reels have one distinct advantage over other brands: In a matter of seconds, the Charlton configurables can be converted, or "configured," from small-capacity reels to larger models simply by utilizing quick-change spools available in several different sizes. No matter what size reel you want, you'll find many in all price ranges, and a little investigation can reveal some gems. To protect the reel while it's mounted on the rod, I usually purchase a high-quality neoprene case.

Fly-fishermen have long debated whether a right-hand or a left-hand retrieve is best. The point becomes moot when targeting small fish, but it becomes increasingly important when chasing large ones. A fly-fisher must have the strength to battle large fish and, more important, the dexterity to retrieve line quickly whenever possible.

Fly-fishers always cast with their dominant hand, but after hooking a fish the hands take on different roles, depending on the angler's preference. Some like to switch the rod to the subordinate hand because they can retrieve line much more quickly with the dominant hand. More ambidextrous anglers find it awkward to change hands after hooking a fish and prefer, instead, to play the fish with the strength of the dominant hand while reeling with the opposite one.

A quick test will determine whether a right-hand or left-hand retrieve

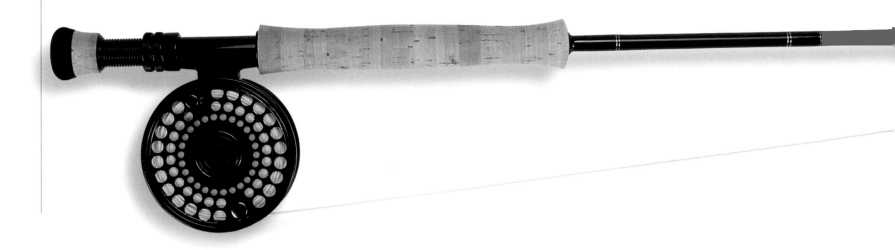

RAFALE STORM LEADER SYSTEM 60/20/20

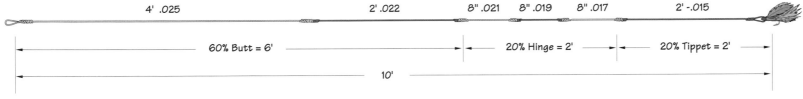

4' .025   2' .022   8" .021   8" .019   8" .017   2' -.015

← 60% Butt = 6' →   ← 20% Hinge = 2' → ← 20% Tippet = 2' →

← 10' →

FOUR-PIECE LEADER SYSTEM 55/20/10/T

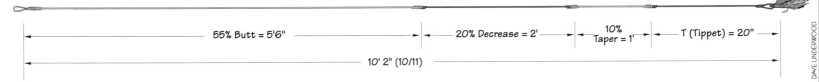

← 55% Butt = 5'6" →   ← 20% Decrease = 2' → ← 10% Taper = 1' → ← T (Tippet) = 20" →

← 10' 2" (10/11) →

DAVE UNDERWOOD

BIG-GAME LEADER

Class tippet   Mono shock

Wire shock

is best for you. With the reel attached to the rod, rapidly turn the reel handle for 15 seconds, first with the left hand and then with the right. This will usually reveal a weakness in the subordinate hand — that's normal. But if you experience a significant difference, as many people do, or if you find sustained reeling difficult, set up your reel for cranking with the dominant hand. If you find the decrease in cranking speed and comfort minor, choose either a right- or left-handed reel.

Another less controversial debate exists between anglers who prefer direct-drive reels and those who like antireverse models. Antireverse eliminates the knuckle-busting knob action that can occur with direct-drive. But one of the trade-offs of antireverse is that you can turn the handle even when a fish is pulling line off the reel. Consequently, an angler doesn't always know if he gains line. On the other hand, direct-drive action leaves no doubt which way the battle is going. One type of reel is not necessarily better than the other, but I believe a fish can be whipped faster with a direct-drive action because it puts the angler in more "direct" contact with the fish.

Leaders and Lines

A fly-fisher should always have plenty of ready-made leaders available, or at least the materials to create them, especially when fly-fishing in remote locations where fishing supplies are limited or nonexistent.

Commercially made leaders have become increasingly expensive, and some don't give the satisfaction that many fly-fishers expect. For convenience and to reduce costs and increase performance, more and more anglers make their own leaders. Hand-tied leaders are actually relatively easy to do if you're willing to spend a little time practicing knots clearly diagrammed in books like *Practical Fishing Knots* by Mark Sosin and Lefty Kreh.

Tapered leaders come in both knotted and knotless styles. A knotless tapered leader proves indispensable around floating aquatic vegetation and debris that might hang up on the knots of a hand-tied leader. But knotted leaders allow customization for a specific fishing situation.

With the advent of nylon fishing line in 1939, Charles Ritz developed the *Rafale Storm Leader System*, better known as the 60/20/20 System. Ritz theorized that the ideal hand-tied tapered leader should consist of three sections: strength, hinge and tippet. He loosely defined the strength (or butt) section as long pieces of heavy monofilament that would make up 60 percent of a leader's length. The 20-percent hinge portion was to consist of short pieces of medium-sized monofilament; and the tippet, a single-piece of the finest mono, would constitute the remaining 20 percent. Using Ritz's somewhat arbitrary definitions, a 10-foot leader for bass or small redfish could have a 6-foot butt, a 2-foot hinge and 2 feet of tippet with the following lengths of monofilament blood-knotted together: 4 feet of 0.025 diameter and 2 feet of 0.023 diameter (60-percent butt section); 8 inches each of 0.021, 0.019, and 0.017 diameter (20-percent hinge); and 2 feet of 0.015 (20-percent tippet). Pound-test can be substituted for diameter, i.e., 40-pound test instead of 0.025, and so on. (See illustration above.)

Ritz's formula may seem unnecessarily complicated, but it does produce

RULE OF 11	
05X	.016
04X	.015
03X	.014
02X	.013
01X	.012
0X	.011
1X	.010
2X	.009
3X	.008
4X	.007
5X	.006
6X	.005
7X	.004

quality leaders. To simplify the leader-making process, I developed a *Four-Piece Leader System* with a 55/20/10/T formula. Using this system, a tapered leader will consist of 55-percent butt section with, 20-percent decrease, 10-percent taper and a tippet section, T, of about 20 inches. The result is a highly effective, easy-to-tie leader. To create a leader with a projected length between 10 and 11 feet long (10/11), the percentages (55/20/10/T) must be multiplied by the shortest length, which in this case is 10 feet or 120 inches. The finished leader would have 5 feet and 6 inches of butt section, (10 x 0.55), 2 feet of decrease (10 x 0.2), 1 foot of taper (10 x 0.10) and 20 inches of tippet (T) for a total of 10 feet 2 inches. An 8/9 leader would have a 53-inch butt section, a 19-inch decrease, 10 inches of taper and a 20-inch tippet for a total length of 8 feet 6 inches.

Big-game or tarpon leaders include a monofilament class tippet section that is joined to a shock tippet. A thick monofilament shock leader is usually enough to prevent break-offs of rough-mouthed species such as tarpon, snook and sailfish. But barracuda, bluefish, mackerel and sharks require a wire shock trace to guard against their sharp teeth.

To insure that any leader turns over properly, it must be matched correctly to the fly. Big, wind-resistant flies require heavy leaders. Light leaders are necessary for gently presenting tiny flies to trout. A mismatched or poorly designed leader can end up a casting abomination.

The thickness, or diameter, of monofilament plays an important role in leader design. Saltwater fly-fishers speak in terms of "pound-test" as an indirect reference to diameter, while trout anglers are more interested in the "X" value.

The X value dates back before the advent of monofilament, when gut was used to make leaders and the "rule of 11" was developed. The rule of 11 comes from the fact that a standard piece of gut had a diameter of 0.011 inch. To make a tapered leader, fly-fishers would run a string of standard gut through one or more of a series of progressively smaller, sharp-edged holes, each of which would shave off another 0.001 inch. "X" refers to the number of "times" a piece of gut would go through the holes. Thus, gut that was 0.010 in diameter had been pulled through the first hole one time, or 1X. A piece of gut that went into a second hole and had a diameter of 0.009 was called 2X for the two times it had passed through separate holes. Standard gut was given a 0X designation because it had gone through the holes zero times. Today, the same X values are regularly used to describe the diameter of modern monofilament, especially when fly leaders are involved.

Monofilament larger than 0.011, or 0X, has a 0 in front each number. For instance: Diameters of 0.012, 0.013, and 0.014 have designations of 01X, 02X and 03X, respectively. As the diameter continues to increase, so do the number assignments.

The appropriate fly lines for each fish and location have been covered rather thoroughly in "The Waters" and "The Fishes" sections of this book. That being said, fly-fishers should always travel with at least one backup of each line type in case one is damaged beyond use, broken or somehow lost.

Luggage and Storage Containers

Luggage needs vary greatly from trip to trip. Fishermen headed to a populace destination can travel under comparatively few restrictions. Travel to a remote location on a small plane, however, usually requires compact, lightweight luggage that is highly functional and judiciously packed with the barest of necessities. On several occasions, I've had a 25-pound limitation for *all* gear, including tackle, cameras and enough clothing for a 10-day stay.

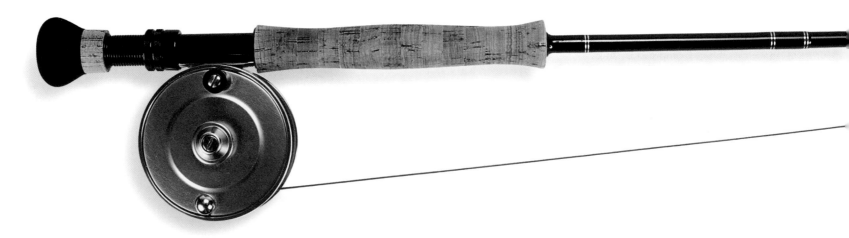

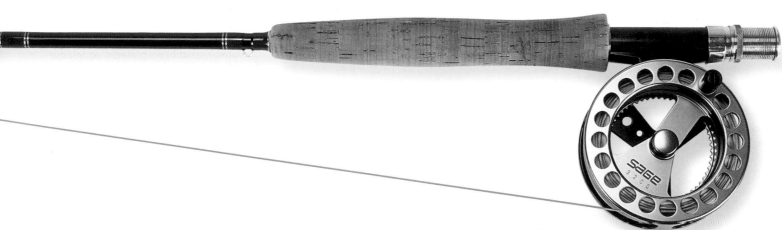

Regardless of the destination and method of travel, I prefer soft luggage over the hard-sided kind. That's because today's cloth materials are extremely puncture-resistant and have the added feature of conforming somewhat to the shape of the load. The best ones feature multiple compartments with rustproof brass or YKK zippers, and I wouldn't purchase any moderate-sized to large piece that didn't have a durable, telescopic handle and high-quality ball-bearing wheels.

For lengthy trips with few luggage limitations, a large duffel is hard to beat. It should have enough room to carry anything a fly-fisher will need, be durable and have several compartments for versatility.

The Eagle Creek Latitude Switchback is my favorite bag for shorter trips or where size limitations exist. As a matter of fact, this little bag holds so much that I frequently use it on long trips as well. This quality backpack/luggage piece has ball-bearing wheels, an extendible handle and padded shoulder straps. Using it as a backpack frees up both hands to handle travel documents and carry additional bags or rods. It also features a detachable daypack that can hold tackle, camera and flies during a day's fishing from a boat. Compression straps allow the attachment of additional rod tubes. Furthermore, Eagle makes an entire line of bags that interact with one another to create a unitized luggage system that is, frankly, unbeatable. As with any quality item, several take-offs of this bag exist.

Since my lightweight carry-on usually doubles as a camera bag that I take onboard a boat, it must be waterproof, padded and have several pockets. To avoid handling several pieces of luggage separately, I also like having the ability to attach the carry-on to the larger bags with straps.

Airline employees who may scrutinize four separate aluminum rod tubes as carry-on luggage may never look twice at a single, larger tube that carries four or more multipiece rods. Dan Bailey's, D.B. Dunn and Boulder River are among the outfitters that offer durable carry-on rod caddies for travel rods.

Liquids should be sealed in small plastic bottles with screw-on lids (available at almost any camping store). Other containers, particularly those made with pop-off lids and pop-up spouts, can leak and may soil clothing and ruin equipment. Breakable containers should be avoided, too. Zip-lock bags in different sizes have a multitude of uses for food, cameras, film, flies, toothbrush, floatant, glue and so on, and they prove invaluable for protecting small pieces of equipment from moisture and dust. Cover larger items with thick (about 1 mil) trash bags that can also hold wet waders and dirty laundry.

While baggage looting usually is not a major problem at airports, it can have disastrous results when it does occur. Small, inexpensive padlocks for latching all openings may not provide a great deal of security, but they may be enough of an obstacle to deter a potential thief. I like miniature combination padlocks because they are sturdy, and there is no key to lose. You can also secure the zippers together using a thick zip-tie strap. These are inexpensive, easy to use and offer reasonable security.

Helpful Hints for Traveling

• A lightweight, multipocketed vest is like a piece of wearable luggage that can carry documents, a book or magazine, snacks, a pen and other items that make traveling easier.

• To avoid dehydration while flying, consume plenty of liquids. Caffeine drinks actually increase the dehydration process and should be taken in limited amounts.

• The effects of alcohol are multiplied when flying at high altitudes.

• Have a pen on hand to avoid delays in filling out paperwork upon arriving or departing from foreign destinations.

• Expensive jewelry may invite theft, especially in poor countries.

Fly-Fisher's Travel Checklist

Preparation for a fishing trip can be filled with uncertainties and questions. Do I need this? Is there enough of that? What if? Travel agents and friends can offer some advice, but most anglers still leave for trips with lingering anxieties. Even with plenty of time to plan, it seems like something is always forgotten. The following checklist isn't meant to rehash the basics of gear selection. Instead, it is intended to aid in the systematic assembly of equipment for a fly-fishing adventure. Just don't forget to turn off the stove when you leave.

Documents
Passport
Vaccination records
Birth certificate
Drivers license
Voters registration
Airline/Train tickets

Tackle
Rods
Reels
Floating lines

Intermediate lines
Sink-tip lines
Sinking lines
Floating shooting heads
Sinking shooting heads
Running line
Leaders
Flies
Mono leader material
Wire
Pliers/Cutters
Pliobond

Fly floatant
Fly vest
Hemostats
Waders
Wading boots
Line cleaner
Line clipper
Backing
Flats booties
Neoprene reel covers
Hook file
Polarized sunglasses

Carry-On
Camera
Film
Batteries
Pen
Book/Magazine

Luggage
Check-in bag
Waterproof carry-on
Rod caddy
Zip-lock bags

Unbreakable bottles
Trash bags
Luggage locks

Snacks
Peanut butter/crackers
Beef jerky
Candy bars

Miscellaneous
Alarm clock (battery type)
Sun screen

Insect repellant
Medicine
Toiletries
Cash
Tip money
Travelers checks
Rain gear
Hat
Glasses
Mini flashlight
Maps/Charts
Compact fly-tying kit

Leave it at home.

• Save luggage space and weight by packing supplex, nylon and cotton blend shirts, pants and shorts. These quick-drying clothes can be washed by hand every few days, eliminating the need to carry extra clothing. I once took a 10-day trip with nothing more than a pair of supplex shorts, two supplex shirts and a pair of nylon pants that I washed every day or so. Everything was dry in less than a half-hour.

• Keep photocopies of legal documents such as your passport or birth certificate in case the originals get lost or stolen. Store them in a separate luggage compartment away from the originals.

• The State Department keeps a list of countries with up-to-date travel advisories and warnings. A brief phone call can help avoid unnecessary risks and ensure a safe trip.

• Information on diseases and the appropriate medications and vaccinations (if available) can be obtained from a county Health Department. Many destinations are extremely safe to travel in, while others have a frighteningly long list of potential hazards. It pays to check and to make the necessary adjustments before traveling out of the country. A case of *Ebola* can be a real downer on a fishing trip.

• Although security X-ray machines at most airports supposedly have no effect on film, in a few, rare locations damage can occur. Most security personnel will willingly hand-check film removed from the canisters

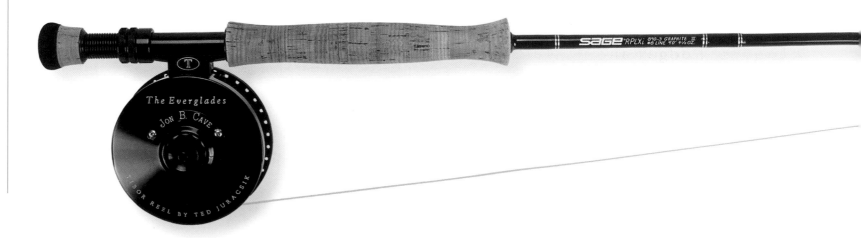

and placed in a zip-lock bag where it is clearly visible. However, some inspectors may insist that the film go through the machine. A specially lined container available at most photo supply stores will allow the film to pass through undamaged.

• Seldom have I been to a location where the food is inedible or marginally so, but it does happen. In one town in Paraguay, a meat market was adjacent to a steady stream of sewage. I asked the driver of my vehicle to identify the large black objects hanging from the ceiling of a local business establishment. "Meat" was the answer. The black coloration was clinging flies, many of which I am sure had recently visited the nearby sewage. Now I always travel with jerky and prepackaged peanut butter and crackers, as well as other snacks.

• Fly rods represent a sizable investment that can end up damaged or destroyed on the rough edges of a boat. Wrapping a wet towel around strategic points will prevent rods from rubbing on sharp edges and will keep them from bouncing around in choppy water. Wet towels also help cover boat cleats and other protrusions that may grab or tangle a fly line.

Guides, Lodges and Travel Agents

Because the telephone numbers, addresses and e-mail addresses of guides and lodges change frequently, I have intentionally omitted them from this book. More current sources include Internet Web pages and advertisements in fishing periodicals, where many of the best fly-fishing services maintain a presence. Fly shops can also prove an excellent resource for finding local fly-fishing guides.

Having worked as a guide for many years, I know how important it is for the client to have an enjoyable time on the water. Of course, catching fish is the top priority, but the trip can be miserable if the guide has a surly or arrogant demeanor. Another problem can arise if the guide specializes in baitfishing or spin fishing and is unfamiliar with the intricacies of fly-fishing. To avoid such situations, ask a guide for a short list of references you can contact before booking.

One of the easiest ways to arrange a trip, especially to a foreign destination, is to use a travel agent who specializes in fly-fishing adventure travel. Consider this agent's experience and reputation. I would not advise booking through any representative who has not visited the destination, unless someone you know and trust recommends them. Some people believe they can save money by booking a lodge themselves, but that usually isn't the case. A lodge ordinarily will charge customers the same price that an agency does, but a top-notch travel specialist provides many additional benefits:

• Someone to greet clients at the airport (usually someone who can speak at least a modicum of English).
• Transportation to and from the airport.
• Optimum air travel times.
• Any lodging necessary at layovers en route to the destination.
• Side trips for sight-seeing.
• Advice on peak fishing times.
• A list of appropriate flies, fly tackle, clothing, travel documents, vaccinations and other miscellaneous equipment.
• Custom trips to meet a traveler's needs and expectations.

One thing that travel agents, guides and lodges cannot do is guarantee good fishing. Sometimes the fish are just off the bite, and adverse weather conditions can spoil the fishing. Still, knowledgeable advice combined with friendly and courteous service can ensure a pleasant experience even when the fishing is slow.

INDEX

EPILOGUE

The odyssey continues.

Jon B. Cave